contents

recipes	2
glossary	60
conversion chart	62
index	63

NZ, Canada, US and UK readers
Please note that Australian cup and spoon measurements are metric.
A conversion chart appears on page 62.

skewered lemon prawns

1.5kg large uncooked king prawns
¼ cup (60ml) olive oil
1 tablespoon grated lemon rind
freshly ground black pepper

Remove heads and legs from prawns, leaving shells intact. Cut along the length of the prawn on the underside, without cutting all the way through. Thread prawns onto skewers.
Place prawns in shallow dish; pour over combined oil and rind. Sprinkle with pepper, cover; refrigerate for 3 hours.
Cook prawns on heated barbecue, flesh-side down, until browned lightly. Turn; cook until just cooked through. Serve with lemon wedges, if desired.

serves 8
per serving 7.4g fat; 602kJ (144 cal)

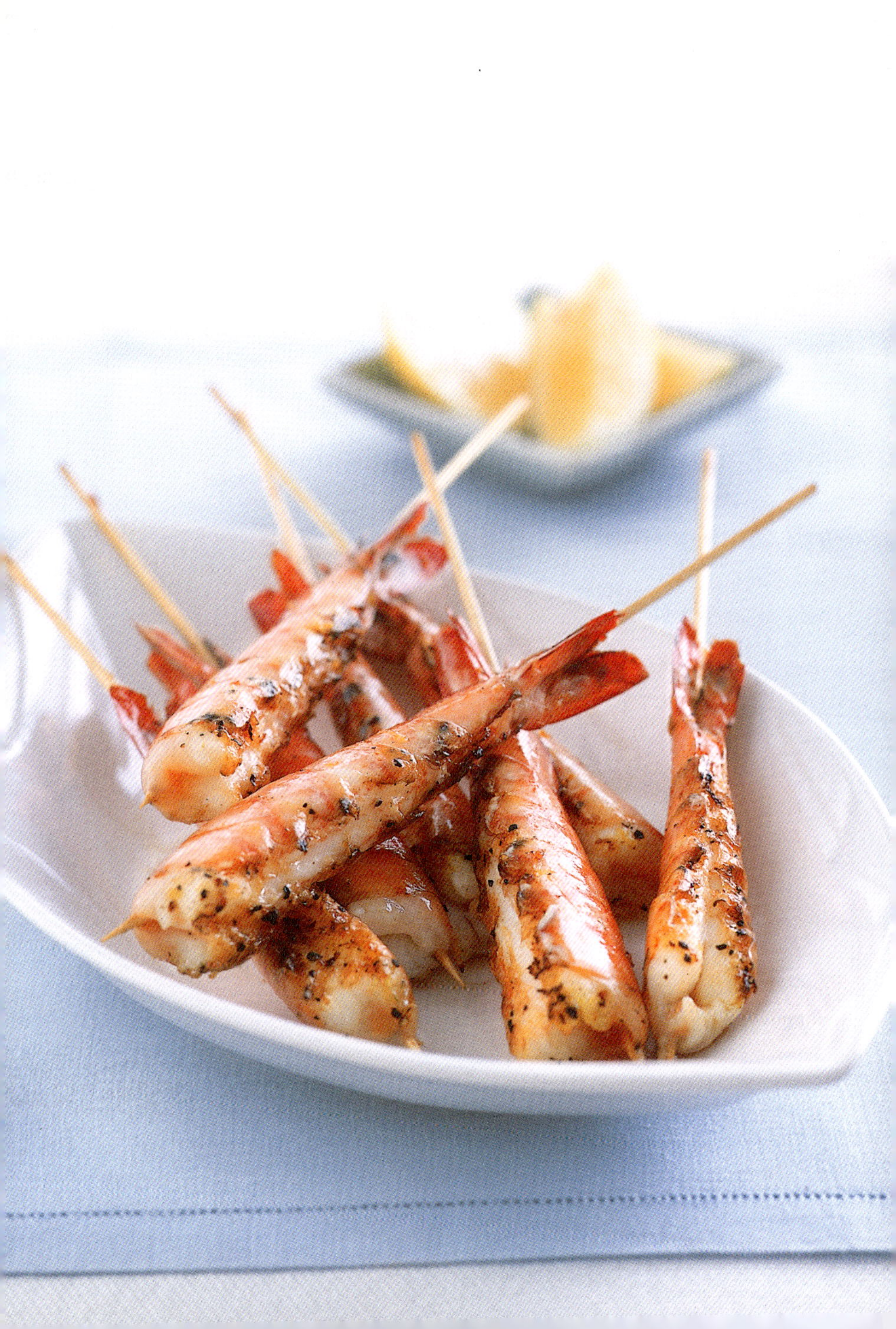

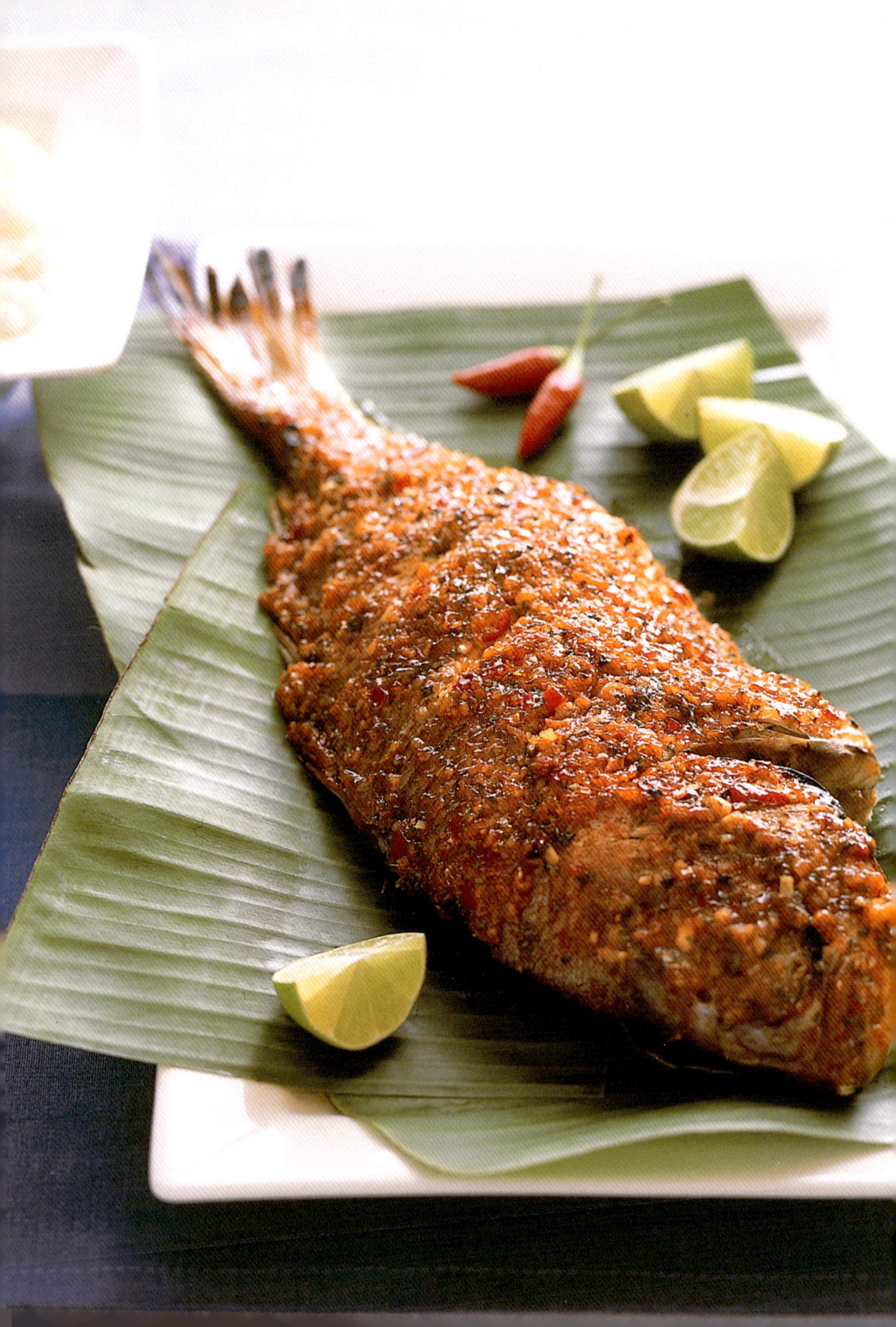

crisp-skinned thai chilli snapper

1.2kg whole snapper
4 cloves garlic, crushed
¼ cup chopped fresh lemon grass
¼ cup chopped fresh coriander
2 fresh red thai chillies, seeded, chopped finely
2 tablespoons mild sweet chilli sauce
1 tablespoon grated fresh ginger
1 tablespoon thai red curry paste
2 tablespoons lime juice
2 tablespoons mild sweet chilli sauce, extra

Make four deep slits diagonally across both sides of fish; place fish in shallow non-metallic ovenproof dish.
Combine remaining ingredients, except extra chilli sauce, in medium bowl. Pour over fish, cover; refrigerate up to 3 hours.
Preheat oven to moderate. Cover dish with a lid or foil, bake in moderate oven about 35 minutes or until fish is almost cooked through.
Brush fish with extra chilli sauce, then grill about 10 minutes or until skin is browned and crisp. Serve with lime wedges, if desired.

serves 4
per serving 4.4g fat; 690kJ (165 cal)

chilli and garlic octopus

1kg baby octopus
2 teaspoons coriander seeds, crushed
¼ cup (60ml) olive oil
2 cloves garlic, crushed
2 tablespoons lemon juice
2 tablespoons sweet chilli sauce
2 cups (40g) trimmed watercress

Remove heads from octopus. Remove "beak" from centre of tentacles.
Heat small dry non-stick frying pan, add crushed coriander seeds; cook, stirring, until fragrant. Remove from heat.
Combine octopus in large bowl with coriander seeds, oil, garlic, juice and sauce. Cover; refrigerate 3 hours or overnight.
Heat grill plate (or heavy-based frying pan or barbecue) until very hot. Drain octopus from marinade; cook octopus, in batches, until tender.
Toss octopus with watercress.

serves 4
per serving 18.2g fat; 1772kJ (424 cal)

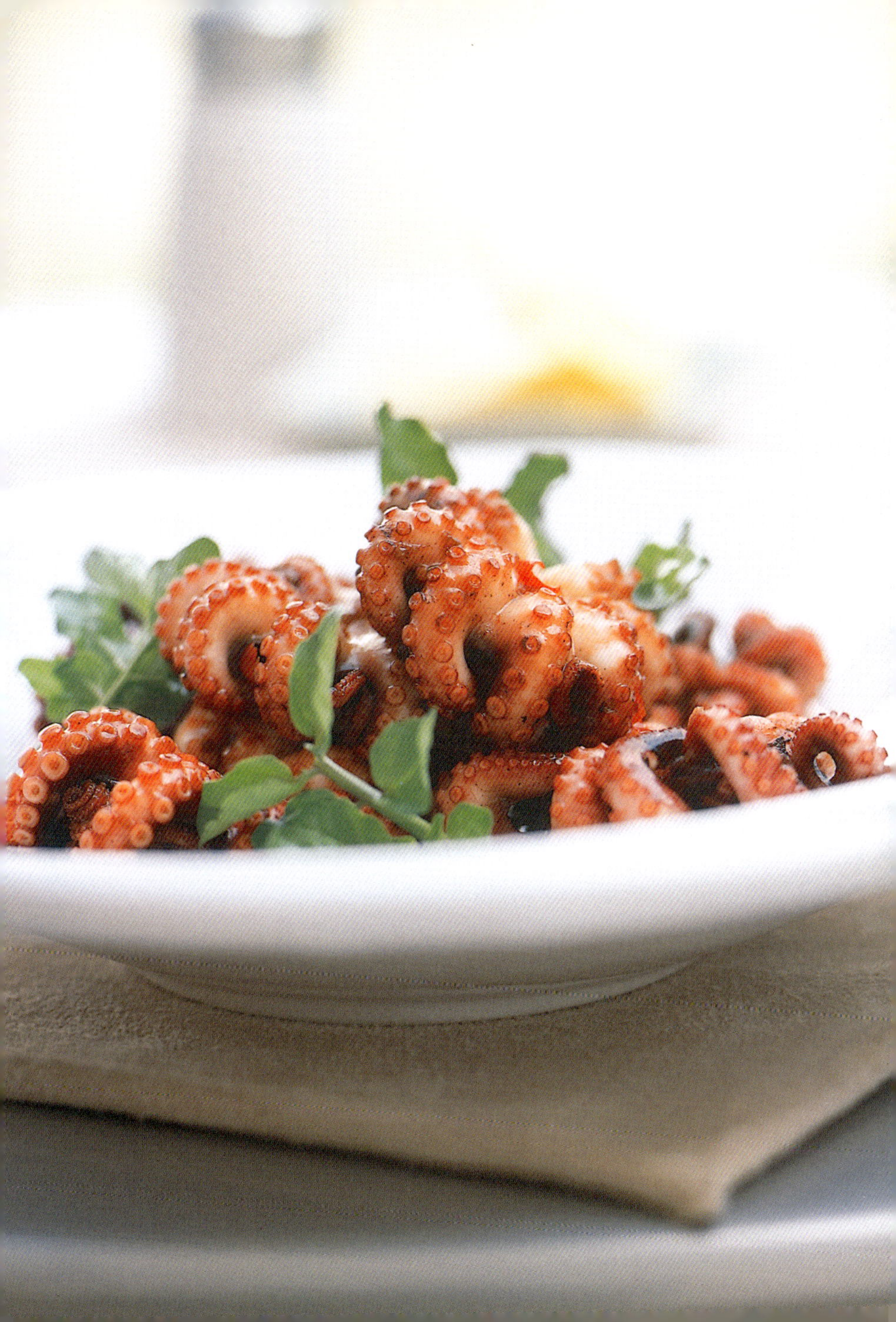

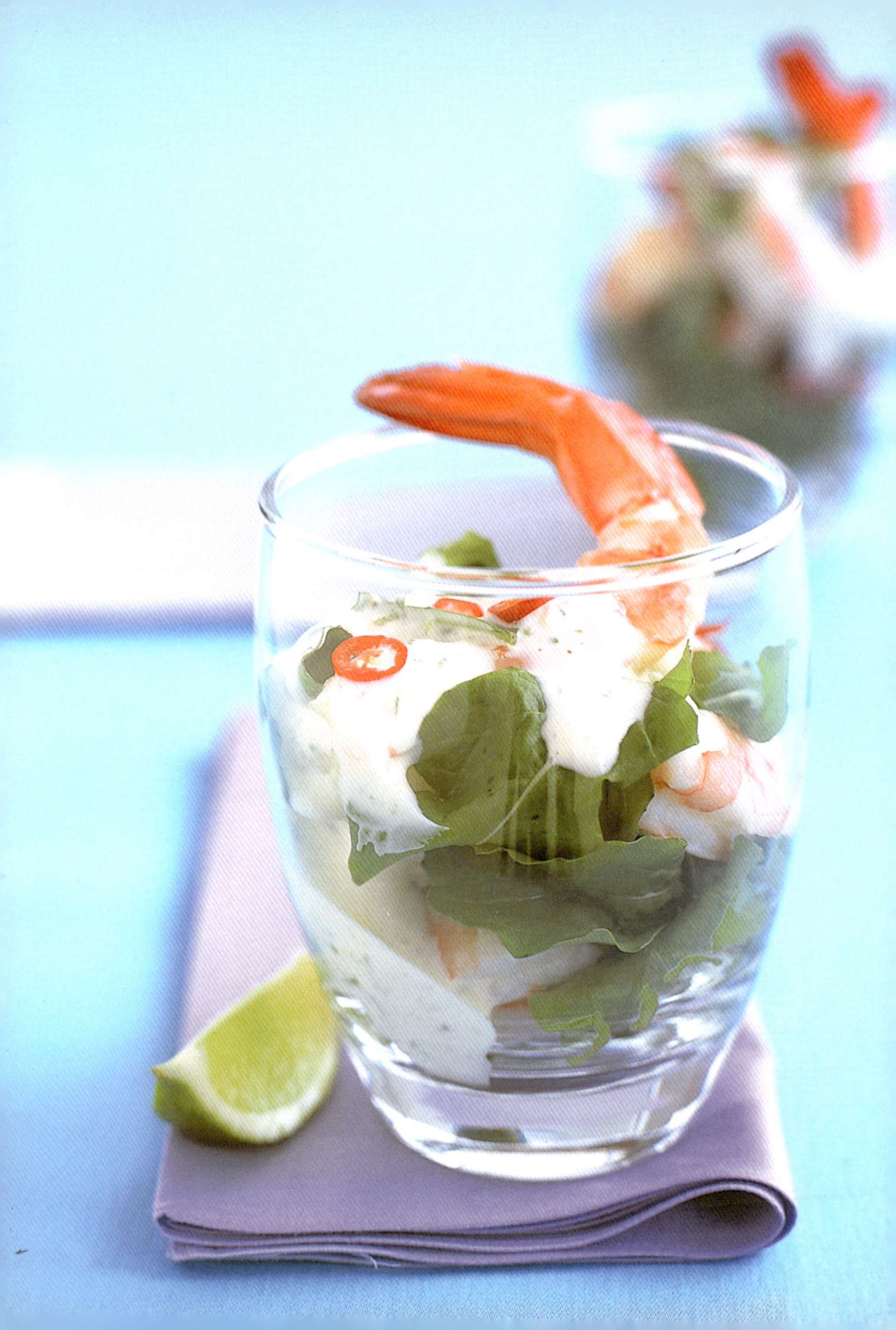

prawn cocktail with lime aïoli

A modern take on the traditional prawn cocktail, this version uses baby rocket leaves rather than iceberg lettuce and replaces bottled cocktail sauce with aïoli, a light and zesty garlic and lime mayonnaise.

1kg medium cooked prawns
100g baby rocket
½ cup (150g) mayonnaise
2 teaspoons finely grated lime rind
2 tablespoons lime juice
2 cloves garlic, crushed
1 fresh red thai chilli, sliced thinly

Shell and devein prawns, leaving tails intact.
Toss prawns with rocket in large bowl; divide among four serving glasses or dishes.
Combine mayonnaise, rind, juice, garlic and chilli in small bowl; spoon evenly over prawns and rocket.

serves 4
per serving 13g fat; 1078kJ (258 cal)

spicy fish kebabs

We've used lemon grass stems as skewers in this recipe because they impart a fresh tangy flavour to the fish; you can use bamboo skewers, if you prefer.

1kg firm white fish fillets
1 tablespoon chopped fresh mint
1 tablespoon chopped fresh coriander
1 tablespoon chopped fresh flat-leaf parsley
2 fresh red thai chillies, chopped finely
2 tablespoons lemon juice
1 tablespoon peanut oil
4 x 30cm-long lemon grass stems

Cut fish into 2cm pieces. Combine fish with herbs, chilli, juice and oil in medium bowl.
Cut lemon grass stems in half crossways; thread fish onto lemon grass skewers.
Cook fish on heated oiled grill plate (or grill or barbecue) until browned all over and cooked through. Serve with lime wedges, if desired.

serves 4
per serving 10.1g fat; 1250kJ (299 cal)
tip If using bamboo skewers, soak skewers in water for a least 1 hour before use, to prevent them from scorching and splintering during cooking.

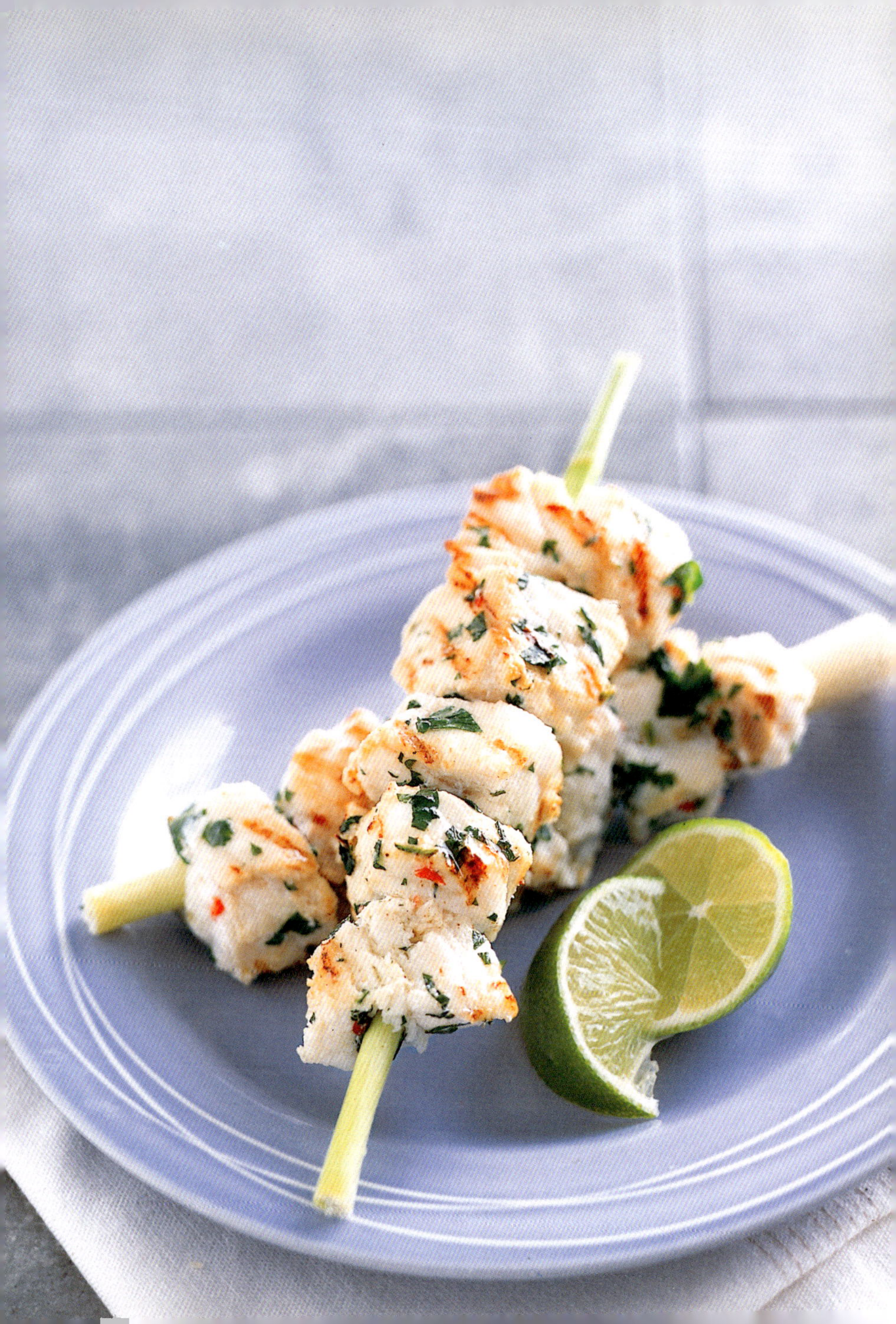

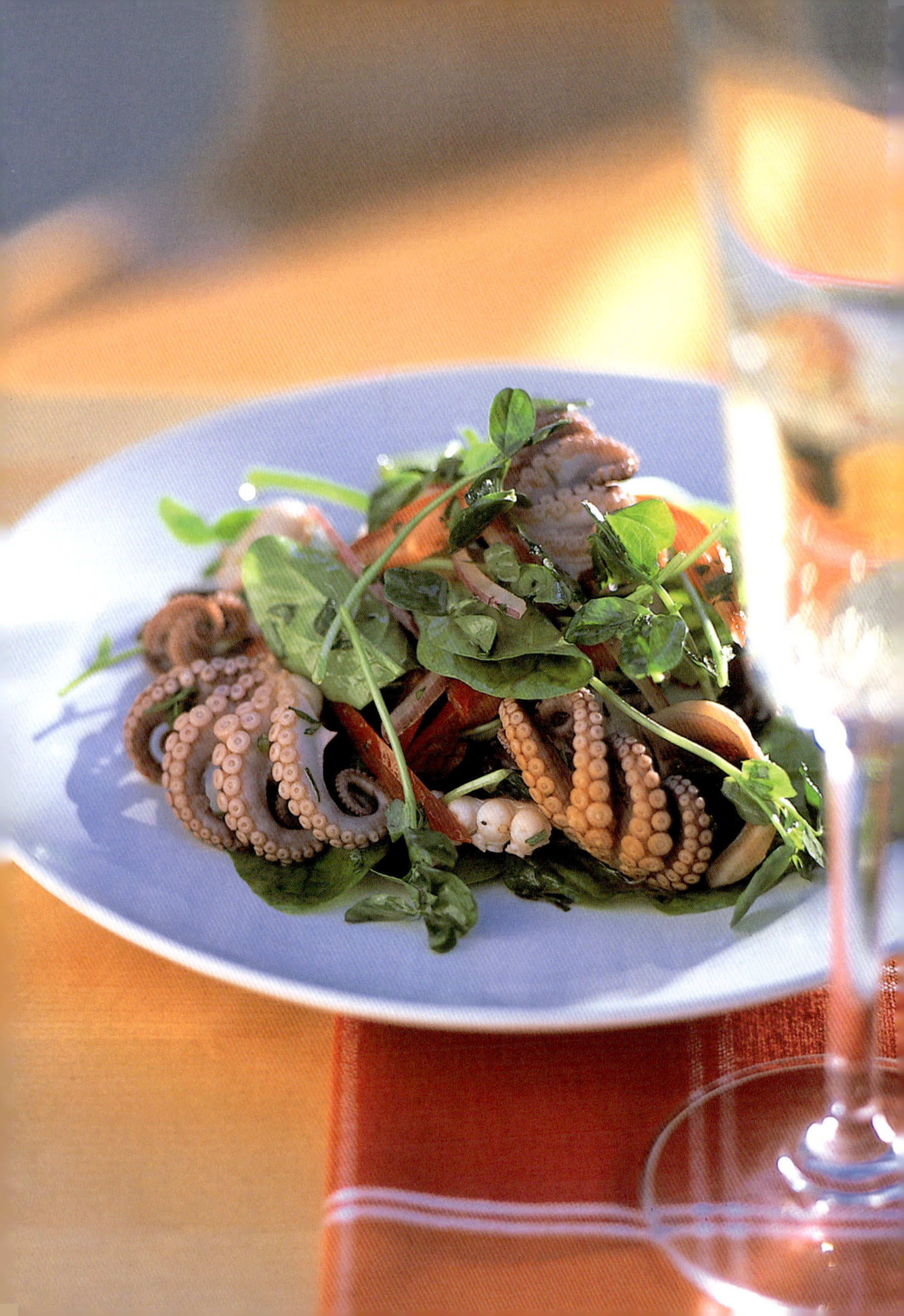

marinated octopus salad

2kg cleaned baby octopus
3 cups (750ml) water
3 cups (750ml) dry white wine
4 sprigs fresh flat-leaf parsley
3 sprigs fresh oregano
2 bay leaves
100g snow pea sprouts
150g baby spinach leaves
4 medium egg tomatoes (300g), seeded, sliced thinly
1 medium red onion (170g), sliced thinly
herb dressing
1 cup (250ml) olive oil
$2/3$ cup (160ml) lemon juice
2 cloves garlic, crushed
$2/3$ cup chopped fresh flat-leaf parsley
2 tablespoons chopped fresh oregano
$1/4$ cup (60ml) balsamic vinegar

Cut octopus in half; combine with the water, wine, herbs and bay leaves in large saucepan. Bring to a boil; simmer, covered, about 15 minutes or until octopus is tender. Drain; discard herbs, cool octopus.
Combine octopus and herb dressing in large bowl. Cover tightly; refrigerate overnight.
Just before serving, add sprouts, spinach, tomato and onion to octopus mixture; toss to combine.
Herb dressing Combine ingredients in screw-top jar; shake well.

serves 6
per serving 43.1g fat; 2997kJ (717 cal)
tip Octopus must be marinated overnight in the herb dressing to tenderise it.

tuna carpaccio with lemon oil and baby capers

400g sashimi tuna, sliced thinly
1 tablespoon extra virgin olive oil
¼ cup (50g) drained baby capers
2 tablespoons finely shredded lemon rind
2 tablespoons extra virgin olive oil, extra
1 tablespoon chopped fresh flat-leaf parsley

Using a meat mallet, pound tuna between sheets of plastic wrap until paper-thin; arrange on serving plates.
Heat oil in small frying pan; cook capers, stirring, until crisp. Drain on absorbent paper.
Combine rind with extra oil in small jug; drizzle over tuna. Serve tuna sprinkled with capers and parsley.

serves 6
per serving 14.1g fat; 1354kJ (324 cal)

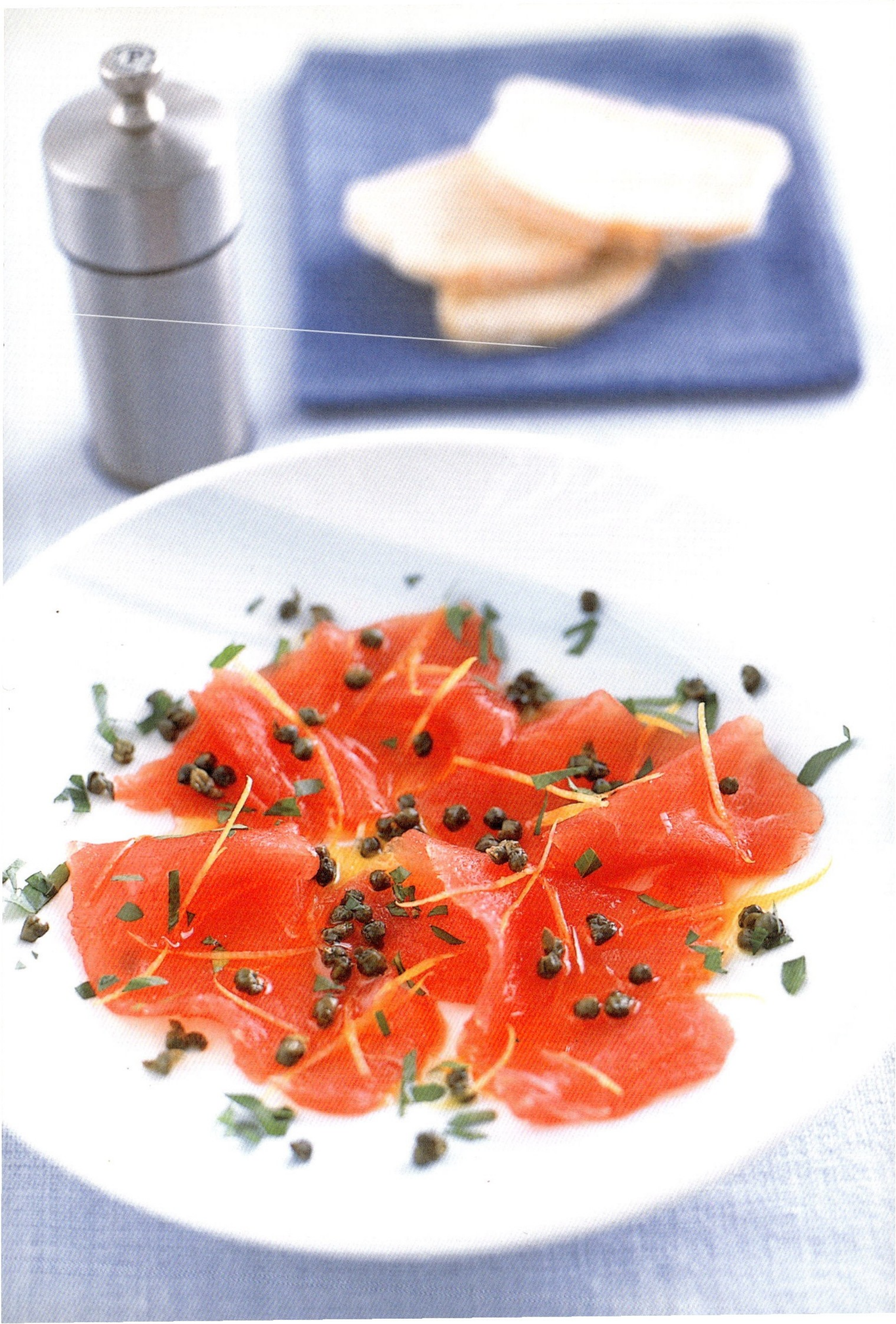

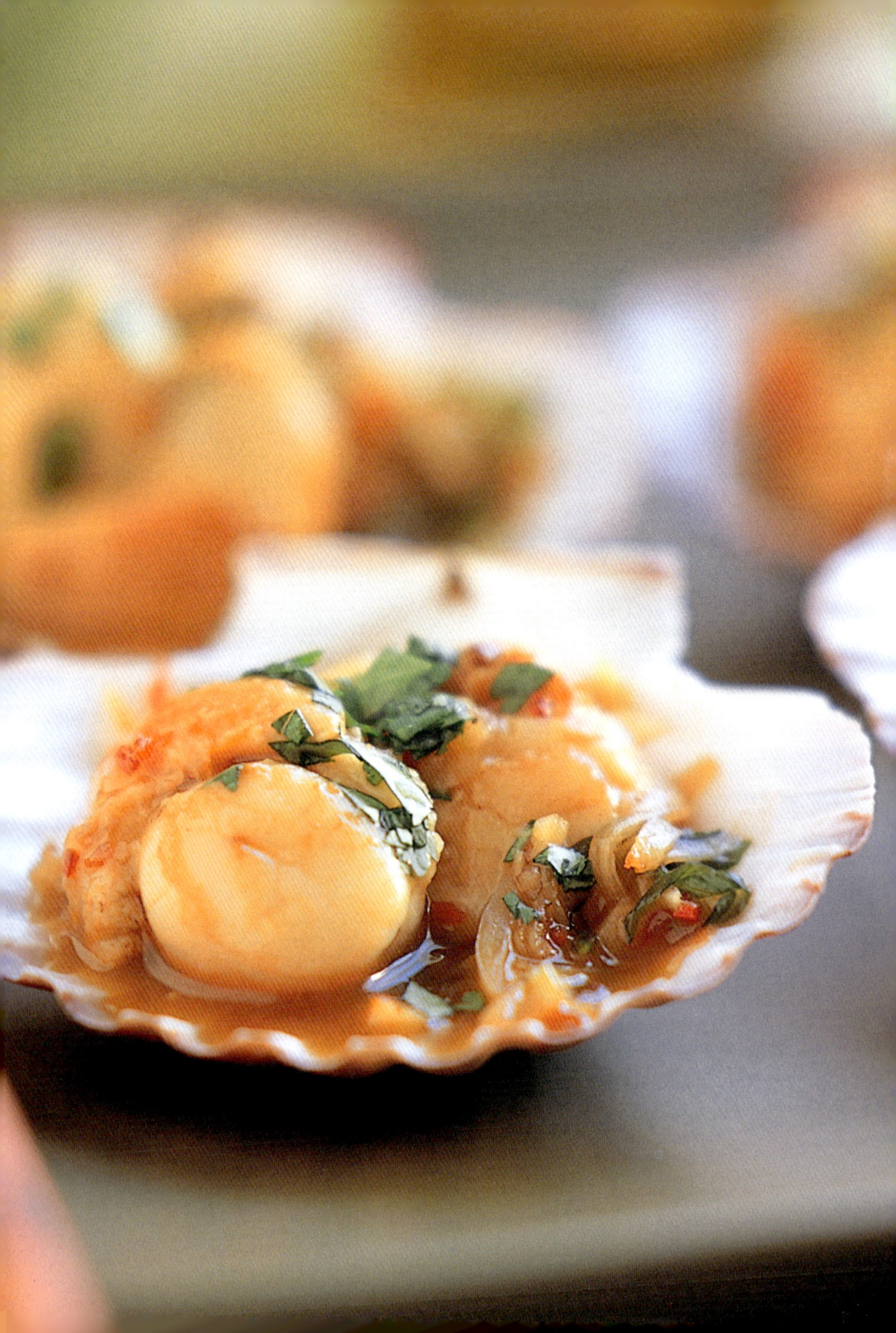

chilli scallops

We used scallops with roe in this recipe; the roe can be removed from scallops, if you prefer. You will need a piece of ginger about 5cm long for this recipe.

1 tablespoon peanut oil
32 small scallops
4 cloves garlic, sliced thinly
50g fresh ginger, peeled, sliced thinly
2 fresh red thai chillies, seeded, chopped finely
3 green onions, sliced thinly
$1/3$ cup (80ml) sweet chilli sauce
1 teaspoon fish sauce
2 teaspoons brown sugar
$1/2$ cup (125ml) chicken stock
$1/4$ cup chopped fresh coriander

Heat half of the oil in wok or large frying pan; stir-fry scallops, in batches, until just changed in colour.
Heat remaining oil in wok; stir-fry garlic, ginger, chilli and onion until onion is soft.
Stir in combined sauces, sugar and stock; bring to a boil. Return scallops to wok; stir until heated through. Serve scallops sprinkled with coriander.

serves 4
per serving 6.1g fat; 585kJ (140 cal)
tip If you buy scallops in their shell, don't discard the shell – they are great (washed and dried) to use as serving "dishes" for the chilli scallops.

chilli prawn and noodle salad

250g medium cooked prawns
¼ cup (60ml) lime juice
2 tablespoons sweet chilli sauce
1 fresh red dutch chilli, seeded, sliced
1 fresh green dutch chilli, seeded, sliced
2 teaspoons sugar
200g bean thread noodles
2 tablespoons shredded fresh mint leaves

Shell and devein prawns, leaving tails intact.
Combine prawns with juice, sauce, chillies and sugar in large bowl.
Place noodles in large heatproof bowl, cover with boiling water, stand until tender; drain.
Combine noodles and mint with prawn mixture.

serves 4
per serving 0.6g fat; 456kJ (109 cal)
tip Red and green thai chillies may be substituted for the dutch chillies in this recipe.

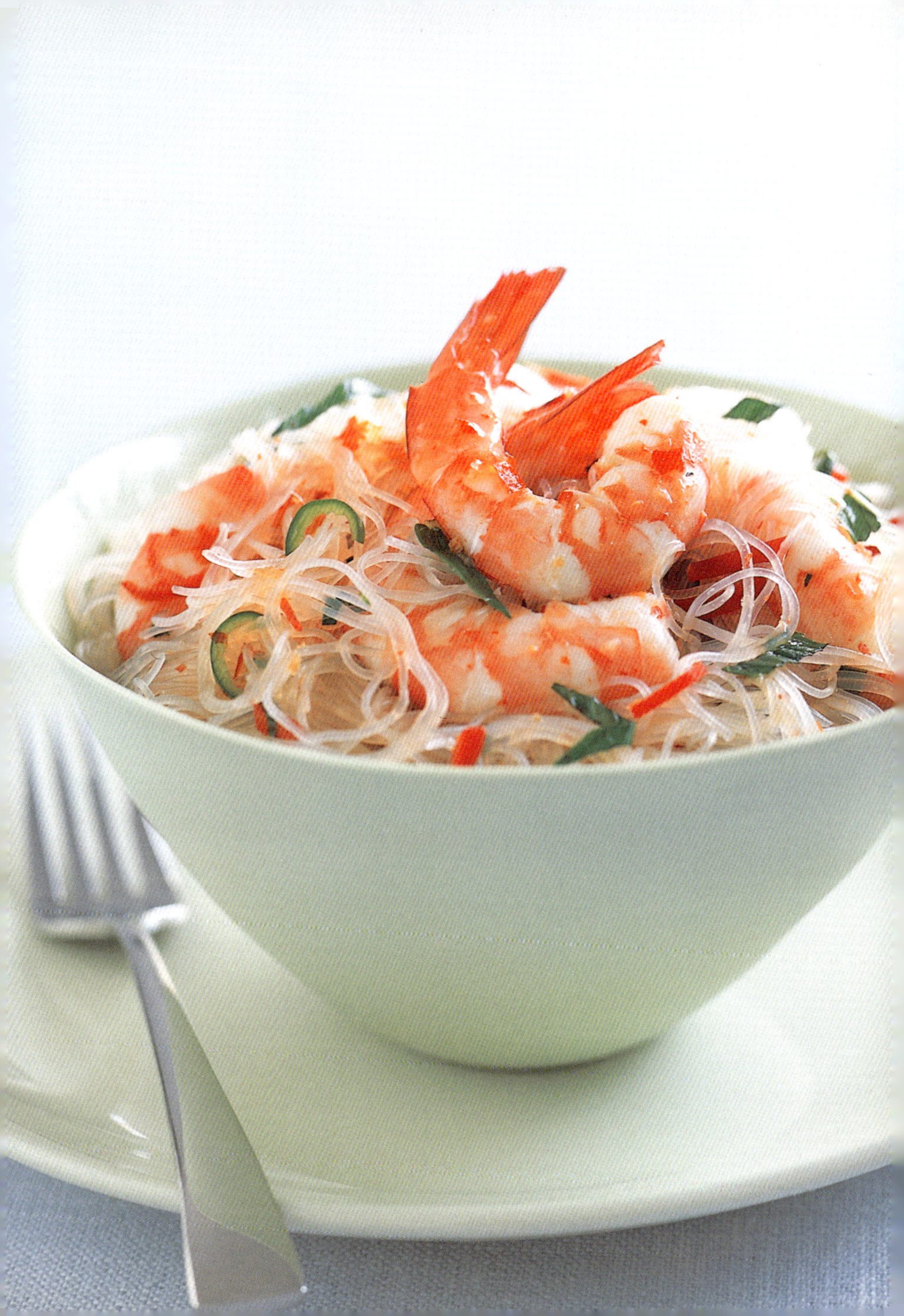

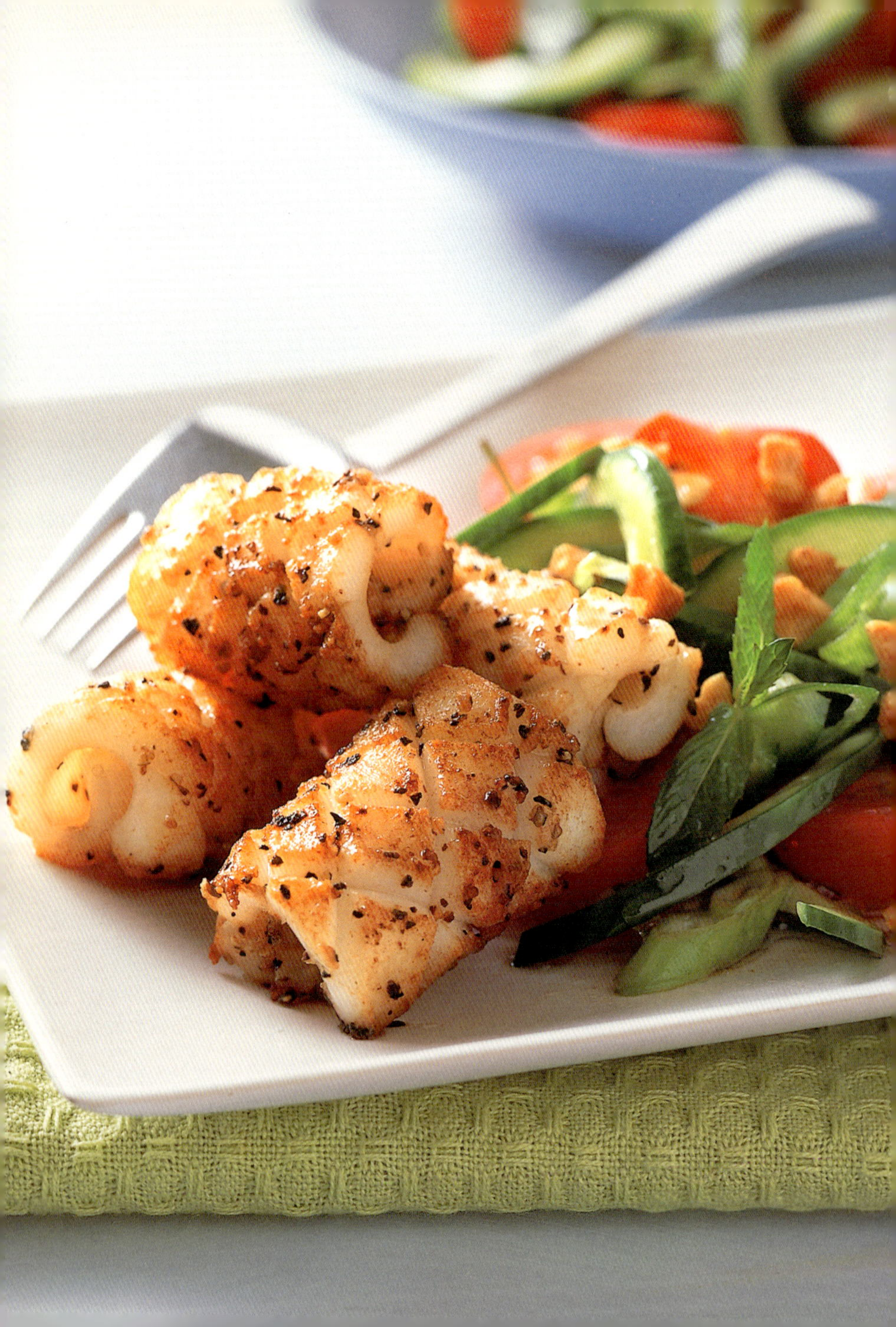

salt and pepper squid with cucumber salad

Ask your fishmonger to score the squid on the inside, to reduce your preparation time.

500g cleaned squid hoods
½ teaspoon cracked black pepper
1 teaspoon sea salt
½ teaspoon lemon pepper seasoning
1 tablespoon peanut oil

cucumber salad
1 lebanese cucumber (130g), sliced thinly
2 green onions, sliced thinly
250g cherry tomatoes, halved
⅓ cup (50g) roasted peanuts, chopped coarsely
½ cup loosely packed fresh mint leaves
1 tablespoon red wine vinegar
1 tablespoon peanut oil

Cut squid hoods along one side and open out. Using a small sharp knife, score inside of hoods in a diagonal pattern, without cutting all the way through (this will allow the squid to curl during cooking). Cut each squid hood into eight pieces.
Sprinkle squid with combined pepper, salt and lemon pepper seasoning.
Heat oil in wok or large frying pan; stir-fry squid, in batches, until curled and just cooked through. Serve squid with cucumber salad.
Cucumber salad Combine cucumber, onion, tomato, nuts and mint in medium bowl. Add combined vinegar and oil; toss to combine.

serves 4
per serving 17.4g fat; 1137kJ (272 cal)

ceviche

While marinating the fish in lime juice appears to "cook" it, be aware that the fish is raw. You will need approximately 10 limes for this recipe.

1kg redfish fillets
1½ cups (375ml) fresh lime juice
¼ cup (40g) canned jalapeño chillies, sliced, drained
¼ cup (60ml) olive oil
1 large tomato (250g), chopped coarsely
¼ cup chopped fresh coriander
1 small white onion (80g), chopped finely
1 clove garlic, crushed

Remove any remaining skin and bones from fish; cut fish into 3cm pieces.
Combine fish and juice in large non-reactive bowl, cover; refrigerate 4 hours or overnight.
Drain fish; discard juice. Return fish to bowl, add remaining ingredients; toss gently to combine. Cover; refrigerate 1 hour.

serves 4
per serving 21.5g fat; 1839kJ (440 cal)
tip Fish must be marinated with the lime juice in a non-reactive bowl (one made from glazed porcelain or glass is best), to avoid the metallic taste that can result if marinating takes place in a stainless steel or aluminium bowl. Ensure all of the fish is completely covered with juice.

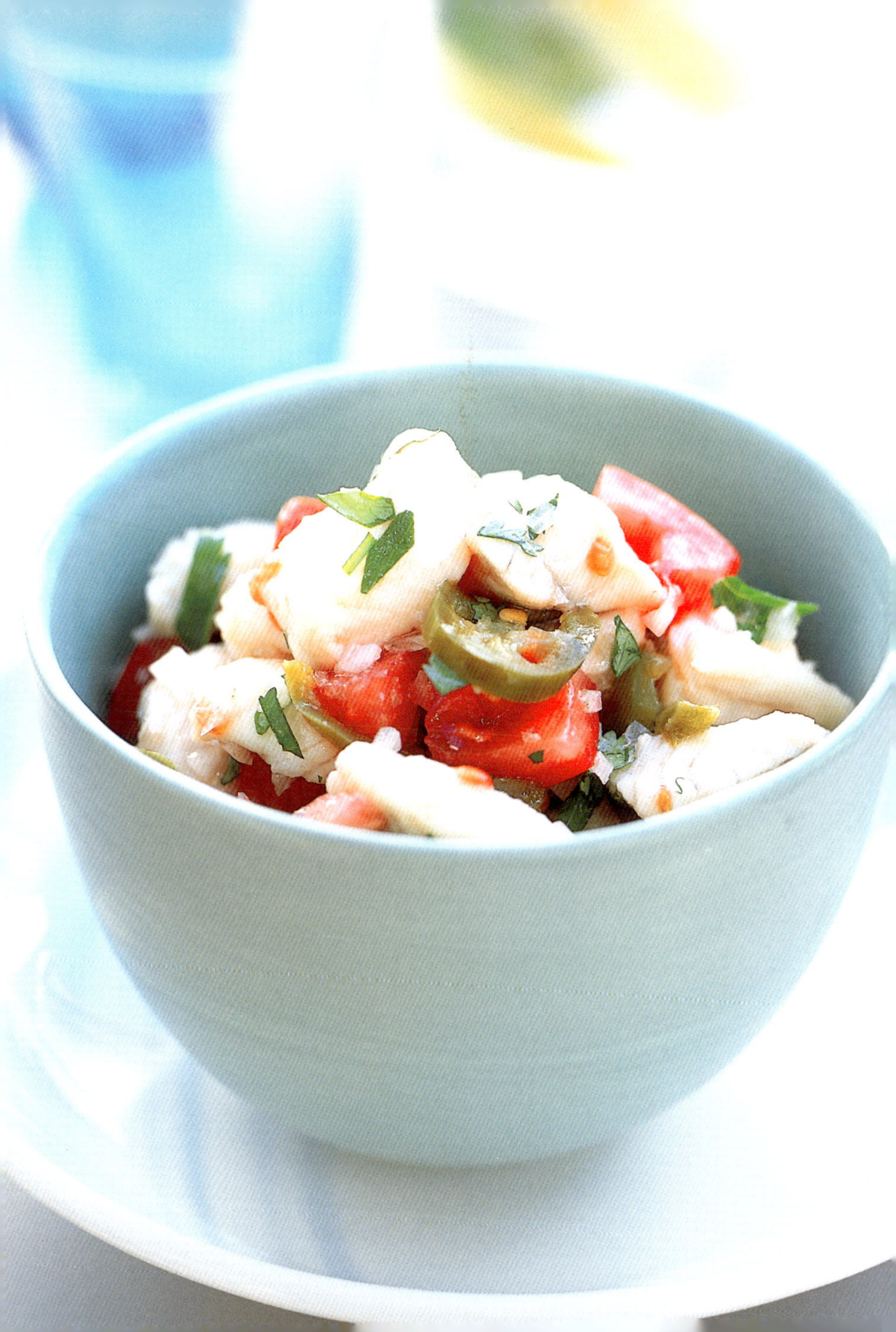

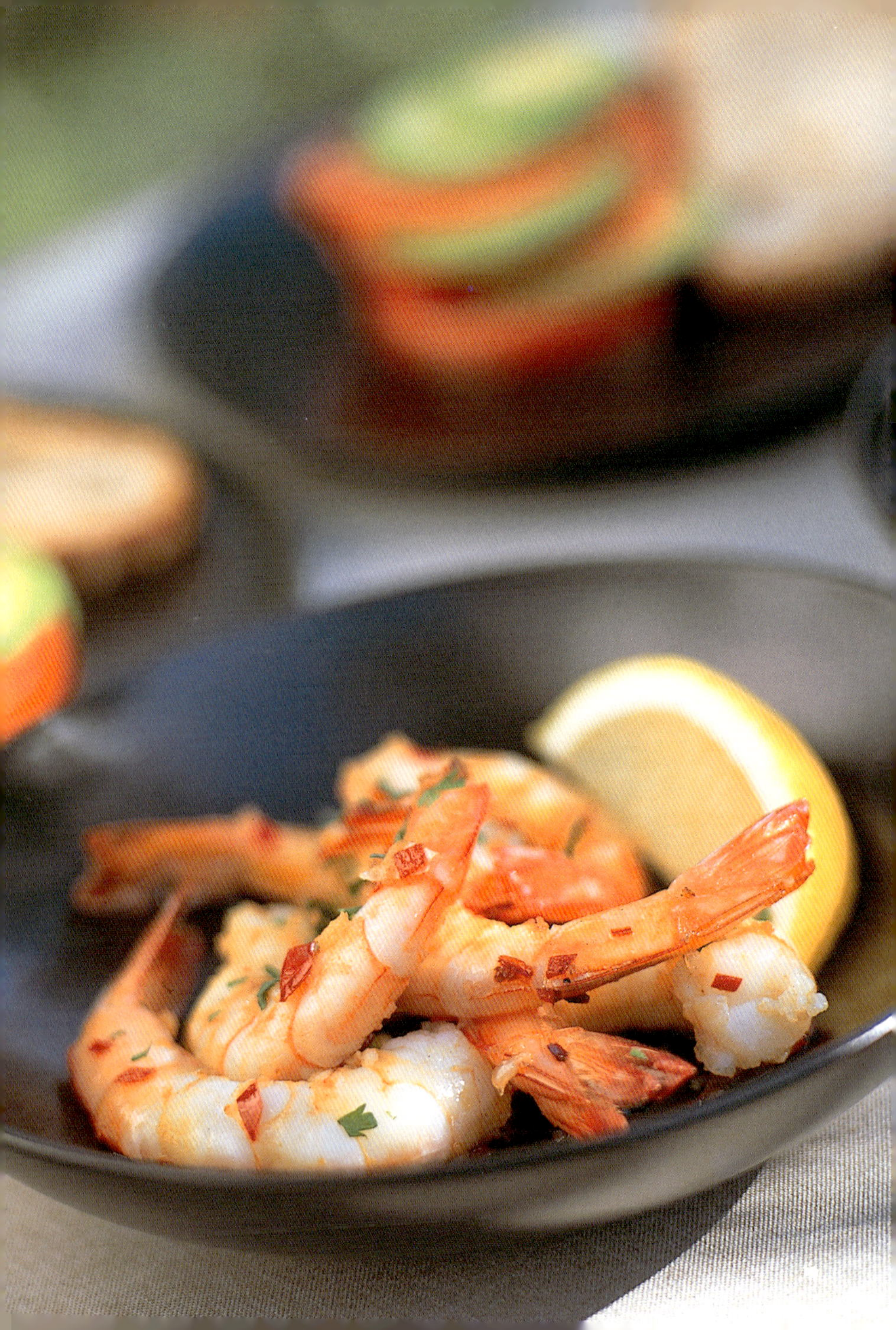

stir-fried garlic prawns

1.25kg large uncooked king prawns
2 tablespoons olive oil
6 cloves garlic, crushed
2 fresh red thai chillies, seeded, chopped finely
2 tablespoons chopped fresh flat-leaf parsley

Shell and devein prawns, leaving tails intact.
Heat oil in wok or large frying pan; stir-fry garlic and chilli until fragrant.
Add prawns; stir-fry until just changed in colour. Serve sprinkled with parsley; accompany with lemon wedges, if desired.

serves 4
per serving 10.6g fat; 949kJ (227 cal)

chilli crab

4 medium uncooked blue swimmer crabs (1.5kg)
1 tablespoon peanut oil
2 fresh red thai chillies, seeded, chopped finely
1 tablespoon grated fresh ginger
2 cloves garlic, crushed
2 teaspoons fish sauce
1 tablespoon brown sugar
¼ cup (60ml) lime juice
¼ cup (60ml) rice vinegar
¼ cup (60ml) fish stock
3 green onions, sliced thickly
¼ cup firmly packed fresh coriander leaves

Hold crab firmly, slide a sharp, strong knife under top of shell at back, lever off shell. Remove and discard whitish gills. Rinse well under cold water. Cut crab body in quarters with cleaver or strong sharp knife.
Heat oil in wok or large saucepan; cook chilli, ginger, garlic, sauce, sugar, juice, vinegar and stock, stirring, until sugar has dissolved.
Add crab; cook, covered, about 15 minutes or until crab has changed in colour. Stir in onion and coriander.

serves 4
per serving 6.1g fat; 807kJ (193 cal)
tip Use shell crackers (like nut crackers) to make eating the crab easier.

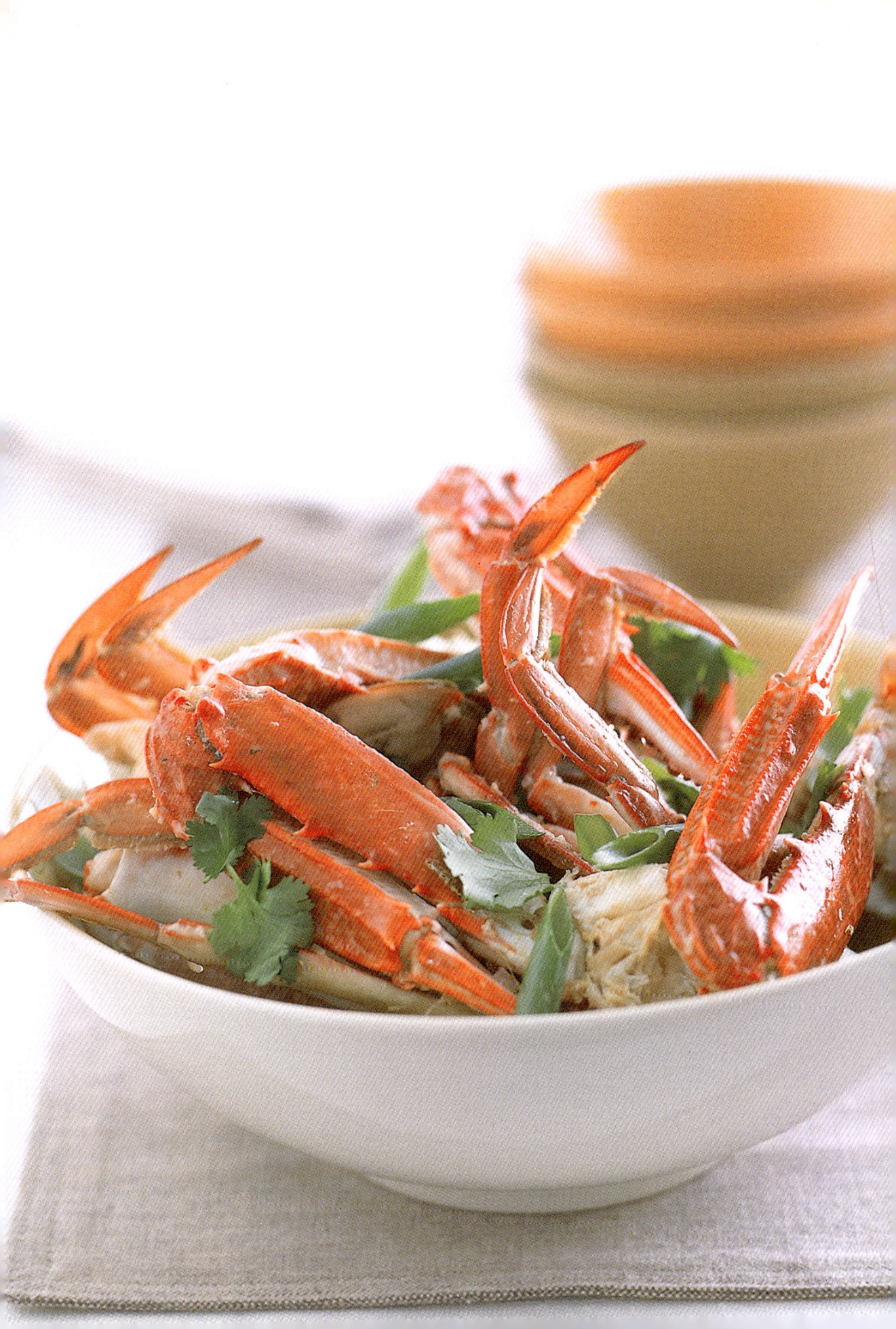

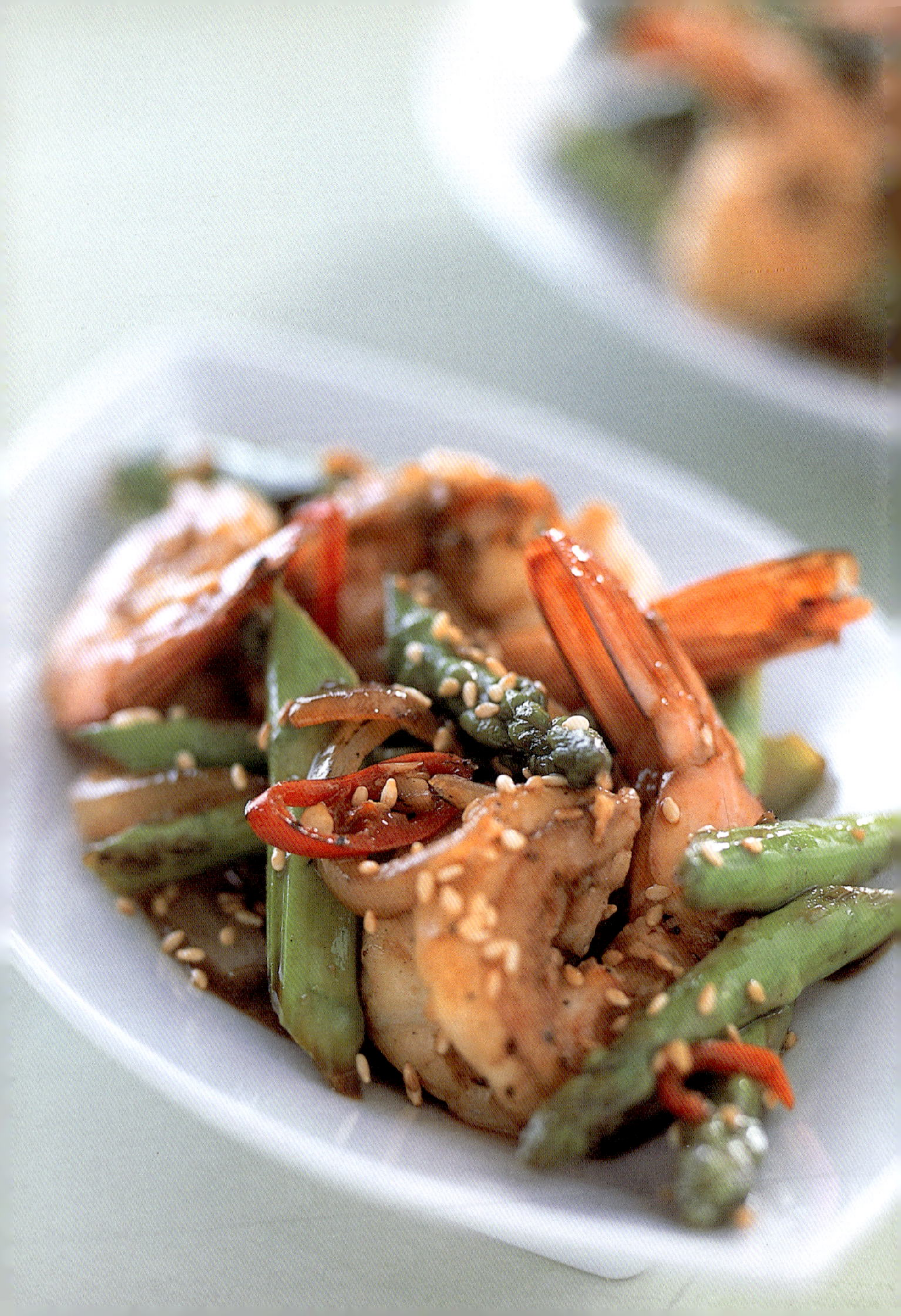

prawn, asparagus and sesame stir-fry

2 teaspoons sesame seeds
1 tablespoon peanut oil
1 teaspoon finely grated fresh ginger
2 cloves garlic, crushed
1 medium brown onion (150g), sliced thinly
300g asparagus, trimmed, chopped
1kg large uncooked prawns, peeled, deveined, tails intact
1 fresh large red chilli, sliced thinly
2 tablespoons rice wine
¼ cup (60ml) soy sauce
2 teaspoons sesame oil
2 teaspoons brown sugar

Place sesame seeds in dry, heated wok; cook, stirring, until browned lightly and fragrant. Remove from wok.
Heat half of the peanut oil in same wok; stir-fry ginger, garlic and onion until fragrant. Add asparagus; stir-fry until just tender, remove from wok.
Heat remaining oil in same wok; stir-fry prawns, in batches, until just changed in colour. Return asparagus mixture and prawns to wok with chilli and combined remaining ingredients; stir-fry until hot. Serve sprinkled with sesame seeds.

serves 4
per serving 8.5g fat; 936kJ (224 cal)

swordfish with coriander pesto

4 swordfish steaks (800g)
coriander pesto
½ cup firmly packed fresh coriander leaves
2 tablespoons peanut oil
1 tablespoon salted roasted peanuts
1 fresh red thai chilli, seeded, chopped
2 tablespoons lime juice

Brush fish with half of the coriander pesto; reserve remaining pesto.
Cook fish on heated oiled grill plate (or grill or barbecue), until browned both sides and just cooked through. Serve brushed with reserved pesto and, if desired, a mixed green salad with snow pea sprouts.
Coriander pesto Blend or process ingredients until well combined.

serves 4
per serving 17.4g fat; 1400kJ (335 cal)

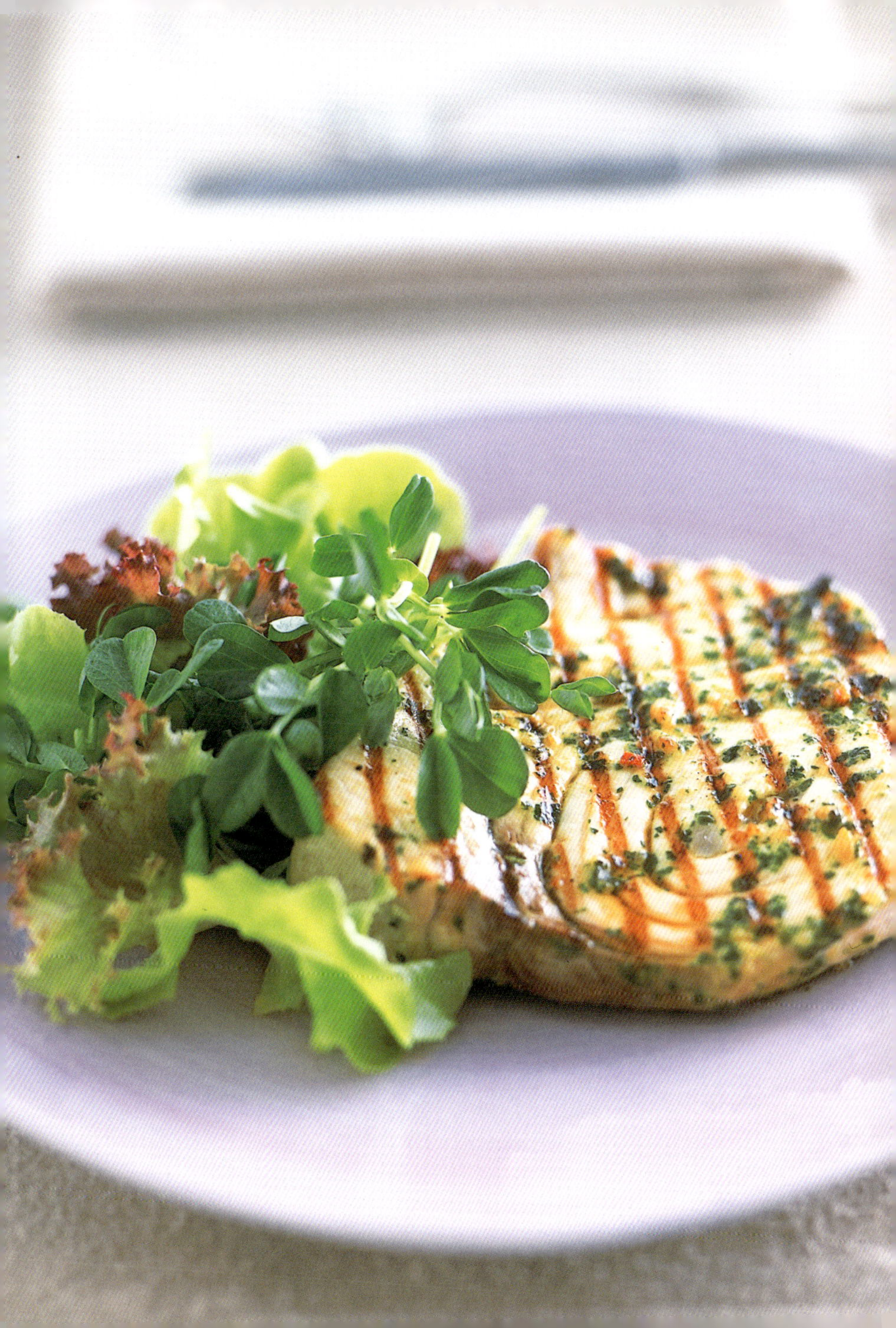

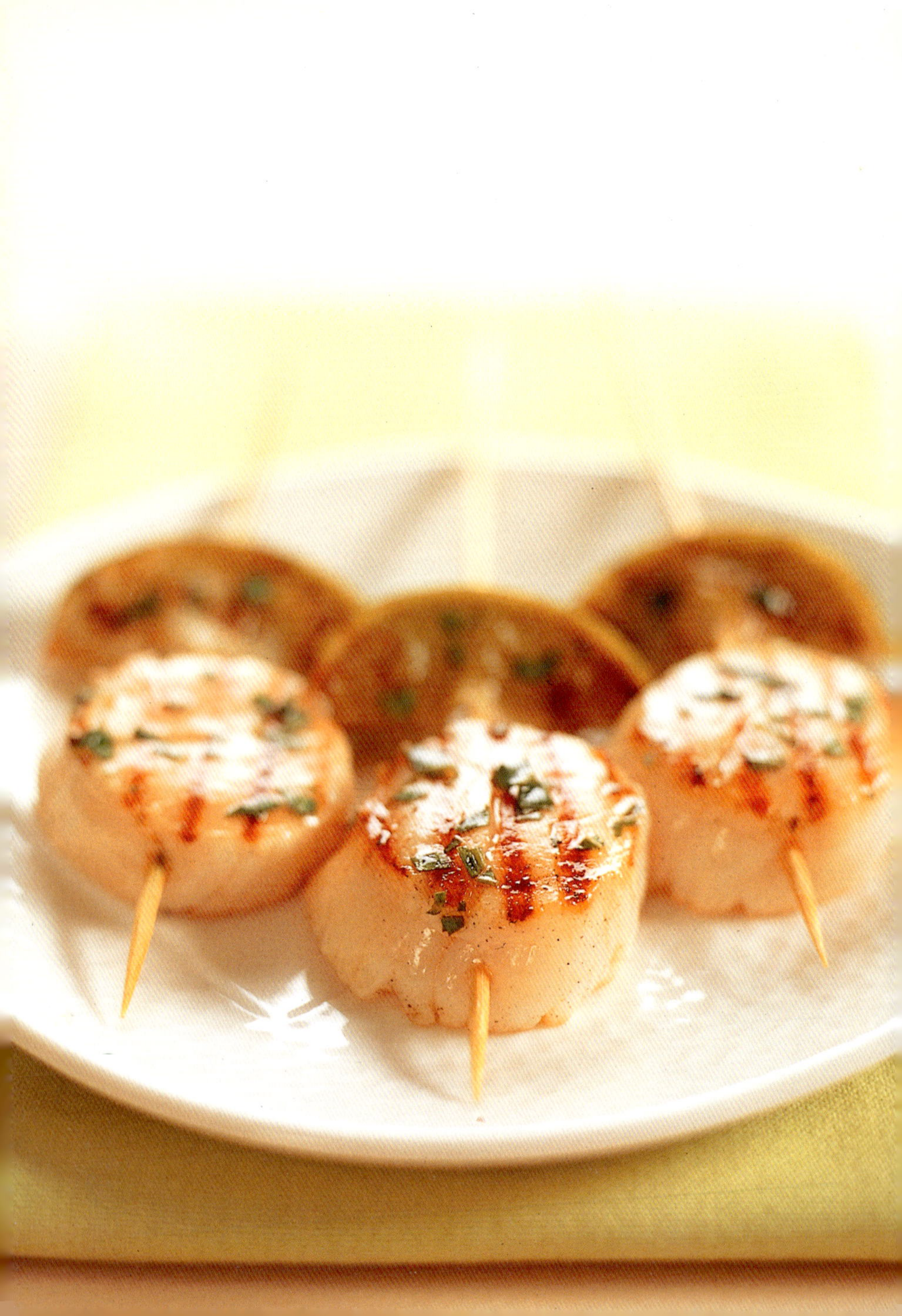

tarragon and lime scallops

24 scallops, without roe (500g)
2 tablespoons chopped fresh tarragon
1 tablespoon lime juice
1 tablespoon olive oil
3 limes

Combine scallops in medium bowl with tarragon, juice and oil; toss to coat scallops all over.
Cut each lime into eight wedges. Thread one scallop and one lime wedge on each skewer.
Cook, in batches, on heated oil grill plate (or grill or barbecue) until scallops are cooked through.

makes 24
per skewer 0.9g fat; 84kJ (20 cal)
tip Uncooked scallops and lime wedges can be skewered up to 4 hours ahead. Cover; refrigerate until required. You need 24 small bamboo skewers for this recipe; soak them in cold water for at least an hour prior to use to prevent splintering or scorching.

prawns with rocket pistou

1kg medium cooked prawns
1 clove garlic, peeled
1$\frac{1}{2}$ cups loosely packed baby rocket
1 tablespoon grated parmesan cheese
2 tablespoons olive oil
1 teaspoon lemon juice, approximately

Peel and devein prawns, leaving tails intact.
Blend or process garlic and rocket until rocket is chopped. Add cheese then, with motor running, gradually pour in oil, in a thin steam, until combined.
Transfer pistou to small bowl, add juice; cover surface with plastic wrap until ready to serve, to prevent discolouration. Serve prawns with pistou.

serves 4
per serving 11g fat; 941kJ (225 cal)
tip Rocket pistou can be made up to eight hours ahead. For a milder pistou, substitute flat-leaf parsley for half of the rocket.

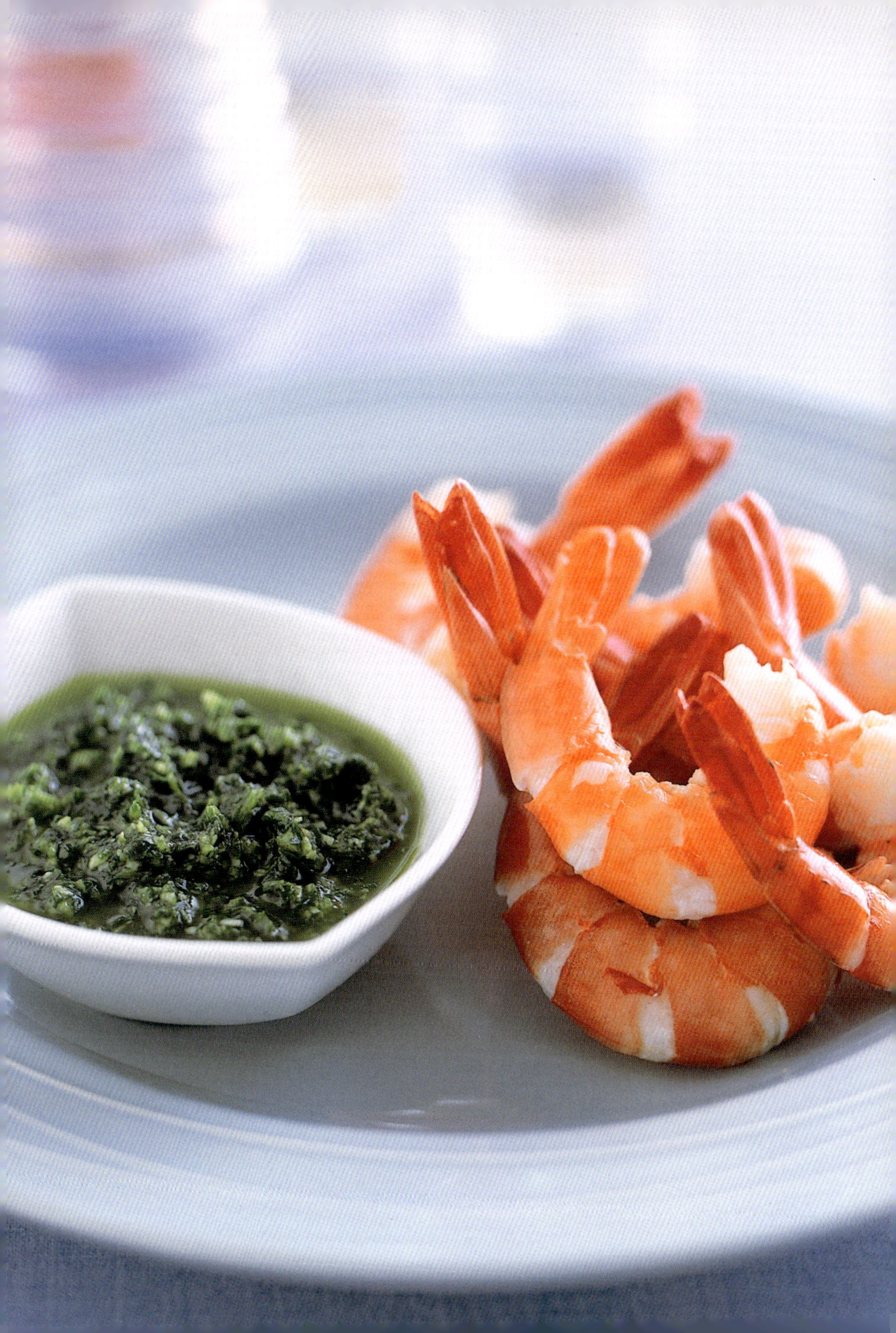

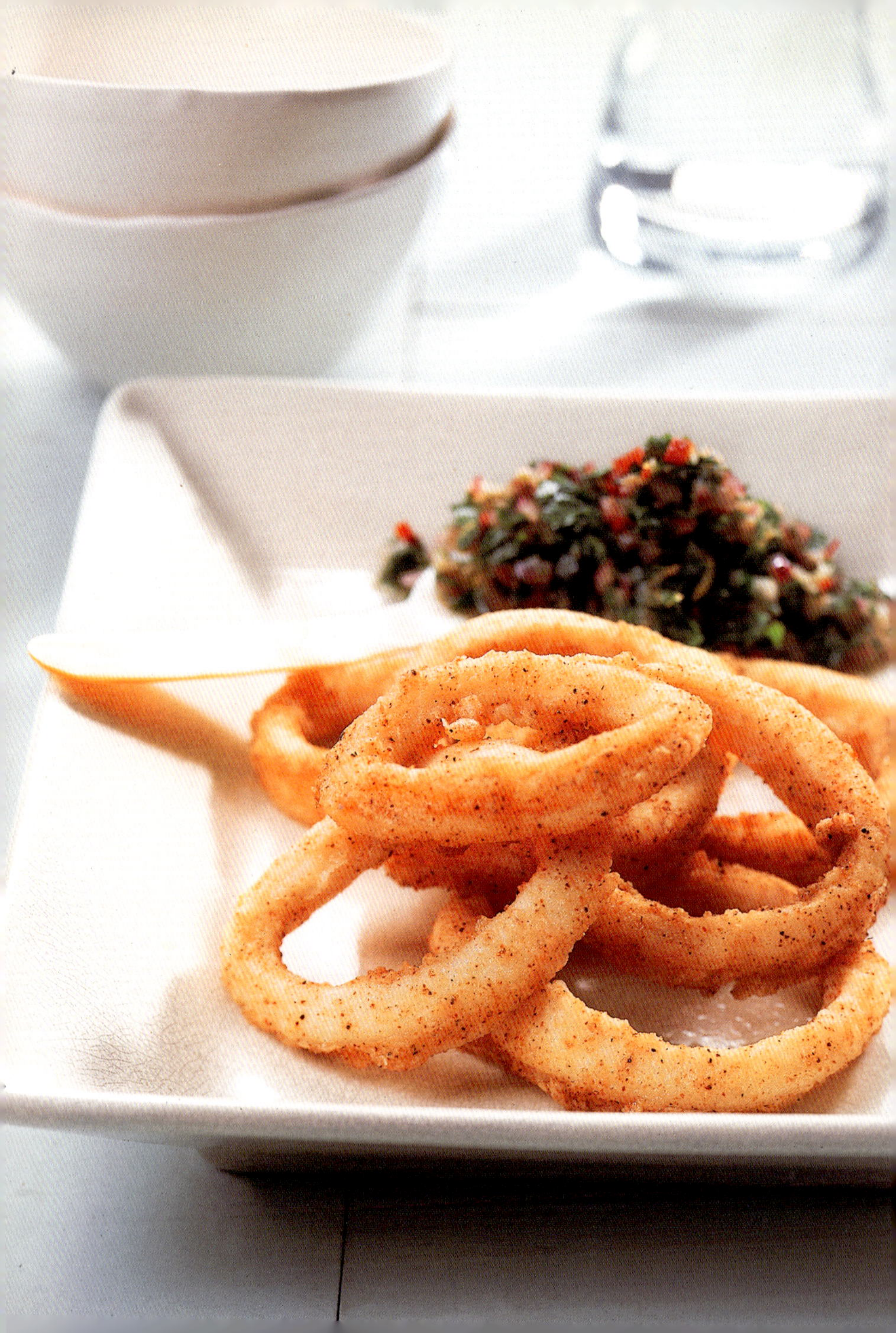

calamari rings with chermoulla

1½ teaspoons chilli powder
3 teaspoons garlic salt
½ cup (75g) plain flour
1kg calamari rings
vegetable oil, for shallow-frying
chermoulla
½ teaspoon hot paprika
1 fresh red thai chilli, seeded, chopped finely
1 small red onion (100g), chopped finely
1 tablespoon finely grated lemon rind
2 cloves garlic, crushed
¼ cup (60ml) lemon juice
⅓ cup (80ml) olive oil
½ cup chopped fresh flat-leaf parsley

Combine chilli powder, salt and flour in small bowl. Coat calamari in flour mixture; shake away excess.
Heat oil in large frying pan; cook calamari, in batches, until browned and tender, drain on absorbent paper. Serve calamari with chermoulla.
Chermoulla Combine ingredients in small bowl.

serves 4
per serving 48.7g fat; 2830kJ (677 cal)

fresh rice paper rolls with prawns

You need approximately one medium carrot and a quarter of a small chinese cabbage for this recipe.

24 medium cooked prawns (650g)
1 cup (80g) finely shredded chinese cabbage
½ cup (120g) coarsely grated carrot
2 tablespoons chopped fresh mint
2 tablespoons chopped fresh coriander
12 x 16cm rice paper rounds

dipping sauce
⅓ cup (75g) caster sugar
¼ cup (60ml) white vinegar
¼ cup (60ml) water
2 teaspoons fish sauce
2 fresh red thai chillies, sliced thinly
1 tablespoon chopped fresh coriander

Shell and devein prawns.
Combine cabbage, carrot, mint and coriander in medium bowl. Place one rice paper round in medium bowl of warm water until softened slightly; lift sheet carefully from water. Place on board; pat dry with absorbent paper.
Place a twelfth of the cabbage mixture in centre of rice paper round; top with two prawns. Fold in sides; roll to enclose filling. Repeat with remaining rice paper rounds, cabbage mixture and prawns. Serve rolls with dipping sauce.
Dipping sauce Stir sugar, vinegar and the water in small saucepan over heat until sugar dissolves; bring to a boil. Remove from heat, stir in sauce and chilli; cool. Stir in coriander.

makes 12 rolls
per roll 0.3g fat; 222kJ (53 cal)
tip Cover rolls with a damp towel to help prevent the rice paper from drying out.

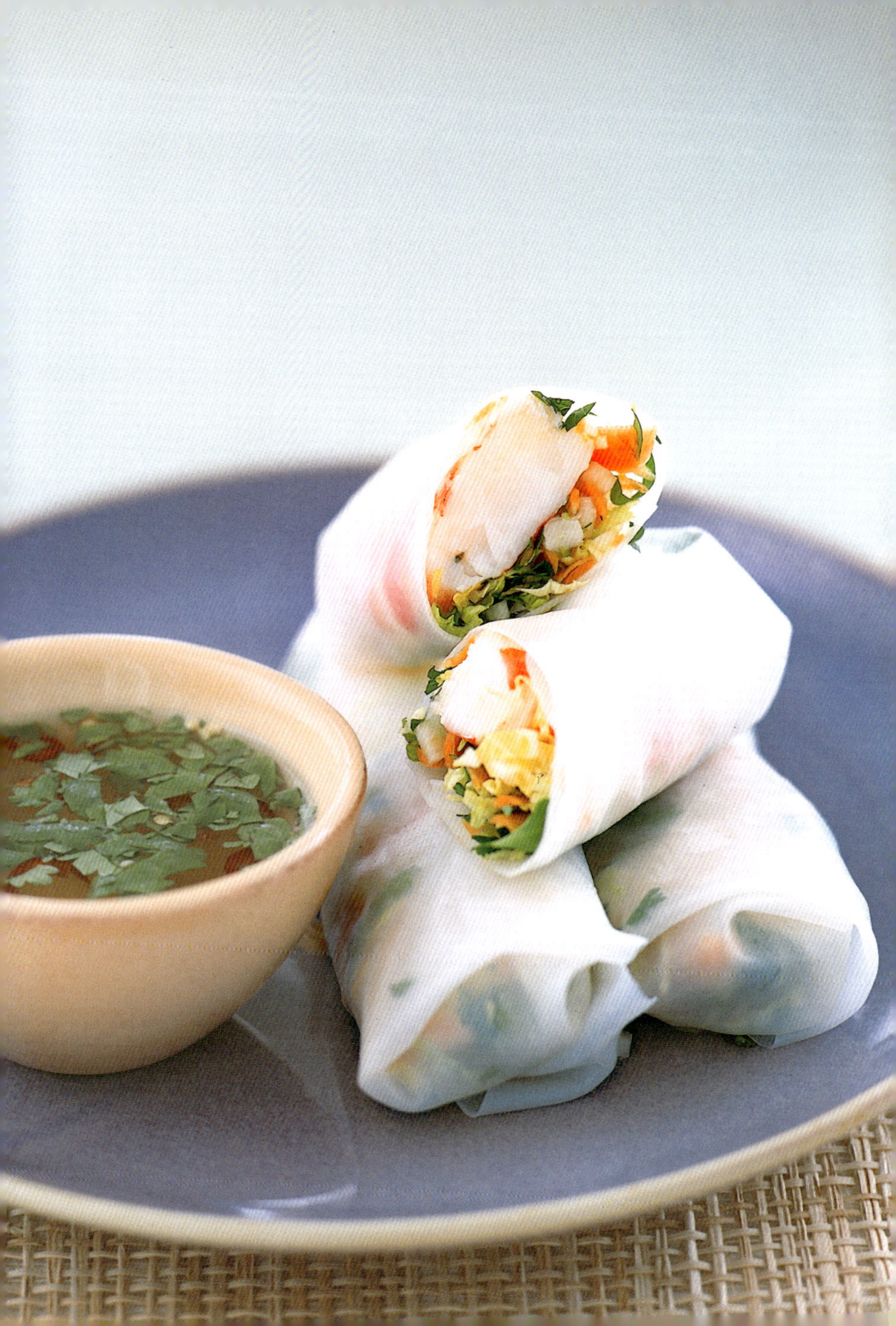

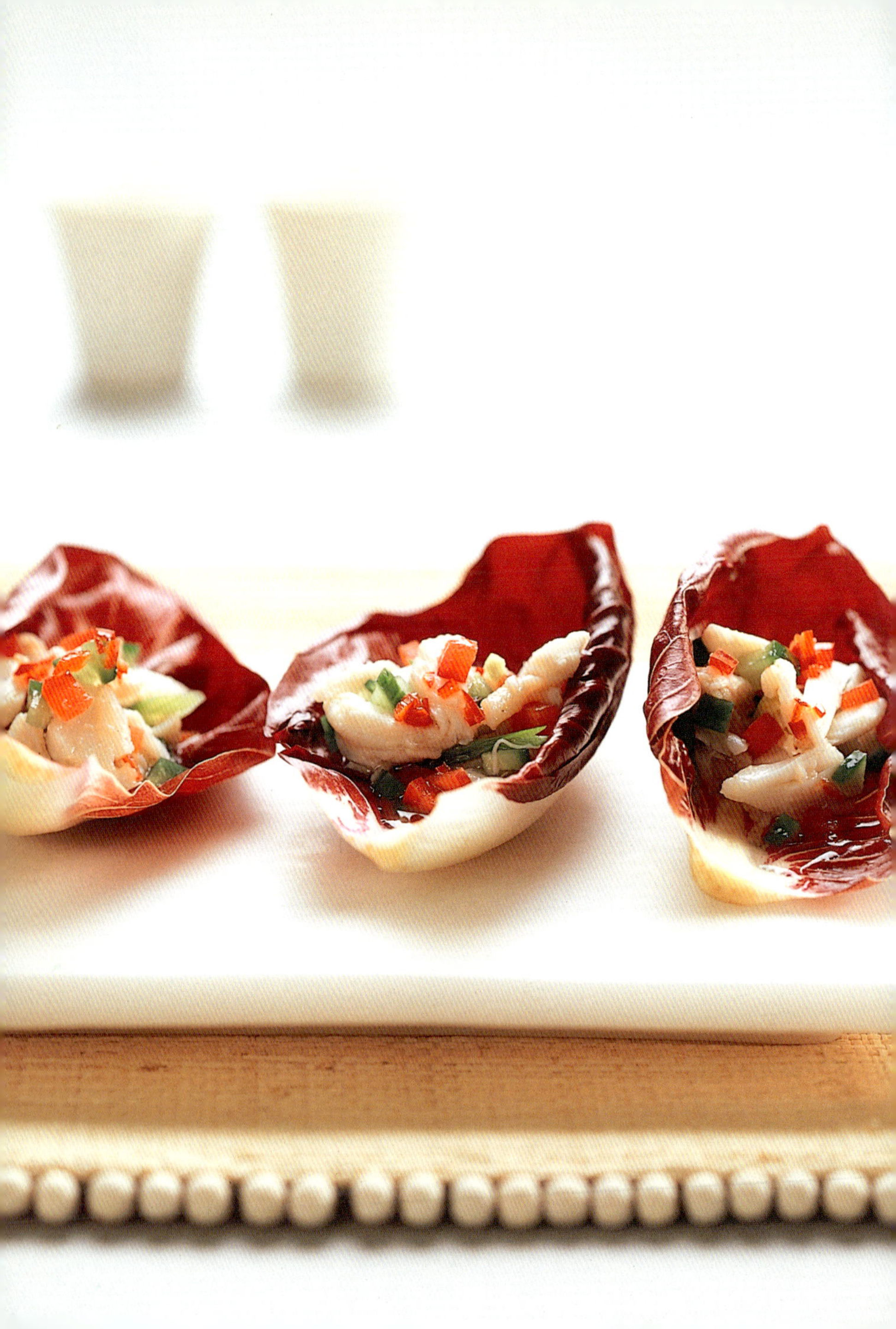

thai crab radicchio salad cups

This recipe is ideal to serve as finger food.

1½ tablespoons water
1½ tablespoons lime juice
1 tablespoon sugar
1 fresh red thai chilli, seeded, chopped finely
250g fresh crab meat
½ lebanese cucumber (65g), seeded, chopped finely
½ small red capsicum (75g), chopped finely
1 green onion, sliced thinly
3 radicchio

Combine the water, juice, sugar and chilli in small saucepan; stir over heat, without boiling, until sugar dissolves. Bring to a boil; remove from heat, cool. Cover; refrigerate dressing until cold.
Combine crab, cucumber, capsicum, onion and dressing in medium bowl.
Trim ends from radicchio; separate leaves (you need 32 leaves). Place 1 heaped teaspoon of the crab salad in each leaf. Serve cold.

makes 32
per leaf 0.1g fat; 38kJ (9 cal)

steamed mussels with chilli and coriander

¾ cup (180ml) dry white wine
1 tablespoon fish sauce
2 teaspoons finely grated lime rind
2.2kg medium black mussels
1 tablespoon peanut oil
1 tablespoon coarsely grated fresh ginger
2 cloves garlic, crushed
3 fresh red thai chillies, seeded, sliced thinly
2 cups loosely packed fresh coriander leaves

Heat wine in small saucepan until hot. Add sauce and rind; remove from heat and stand, covered, about 20 minutes.
Meanwhile, scrub mussels and pull away the beards.
Heat oil in large saucepan, add ginger, garlic and chilli; cook, stirring, until fragrant. Add wine mixture and mussels; simmer, covered, about 5 minutes or until mussels open (discard any that do not). Stir in half the coriander.
Spoon mussels and broth into large serving bowls, sprinkle with remaining coriander.

serves 4
per serving 7g fat; 773kJ (185 cal)

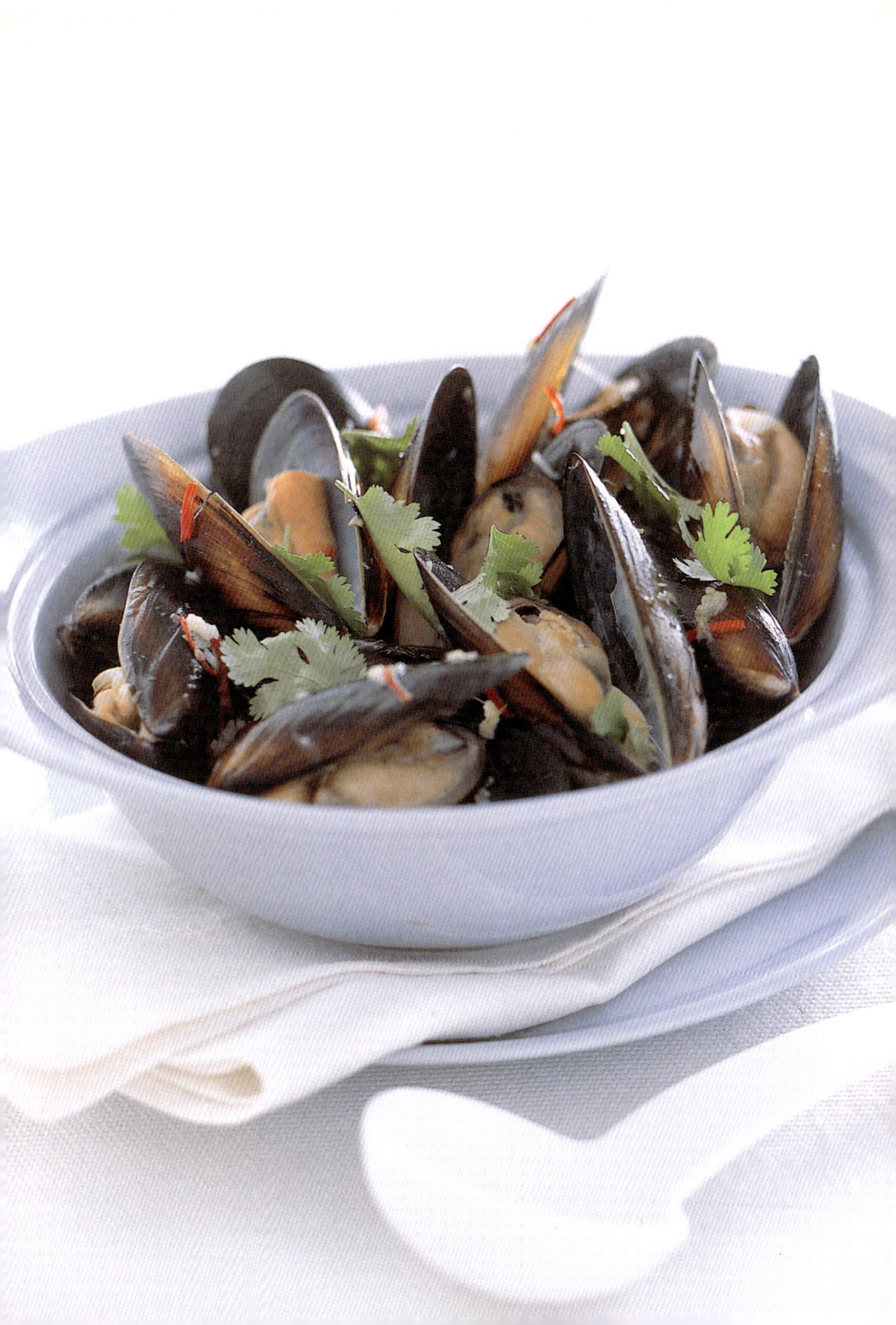

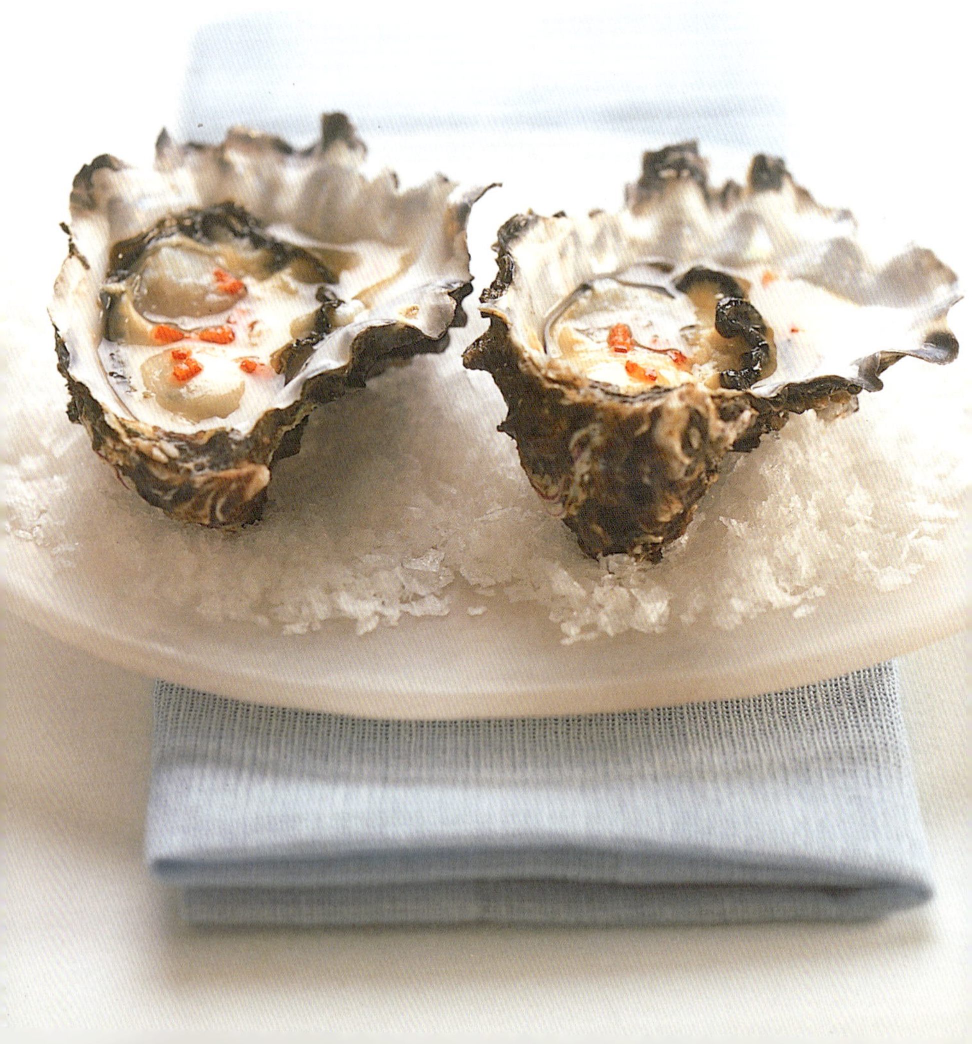

oysters osaka

1/3 cup (80ml) mirin
2 tablespoons rice vinegar
2 teaspoons lemon juice
1/2 teaspoon wasabi paste
2 fresh red thai chillies, seeded, chopped finely
32 oysters, on the half shell
sea salt, for serving

Combine mirin, vinegar, juice, wasabi and chilli in small jug.
Remove oysters from shells; reserve shells. Drain oysters on absorbent paper; wash and dry shells. Return oysters to shells; sit on a bed of sea salt on serving platter. Divide dressing over oysters. Serve cold.

makes 32
per oyster 0.3g fat; 46kJ (11 cal)

chilli seafood pizza

400g whole small
  calamari
400g baby octopus
400g medium
  uncooked prawns
2 cloves garlic, crushed
1 tablespoon chopped
  fresh flat-leaf parsley
1 teaspoon olive oil
1 tablespoon polenta
2 x 30cm-round
  prepared pizza bases
$^2/_3$ cup (180g) tomato
  pizza sauce
4 fresh red thai chillies,
  seeded, sliced thinly
4 green onions,
  sliced thinly
1 medium red onion
  (170g), sliced thinly

Clean calamari by gently pulling head and tentacles from body. Remove clear backbone (quill) from inside body. Remove fins and skin with salted fingers, rinse body. Cut into thin rings.
To prepare octopus, remove and discard head; push black beak from centre of tentacles, discard beak. Cut tentacles into quarters.
Peel and devein prawns. Combine calamari rings, octopus, prawns, garlic and parsley in medium bowl; toss well.
Preheat oven to very hot. Brush two 30cm-round pizza trays with olive oil; sprinkle with polenta. Place pizza bases on trays, spread bases with pizza sauce.
Divide seafood mixture between pizzas. Top with chilli and green and red onions.
Bake in very hot oven 10 minutes. Reduce heat to moderate. Slide pizzas from trays onto oven racks, bake 10 minutes or until bases are crisp. Serve sprinkled with extra parsley, if desired.

serves 6
per serving 6.2g fat; 1873kJ (448 cal)

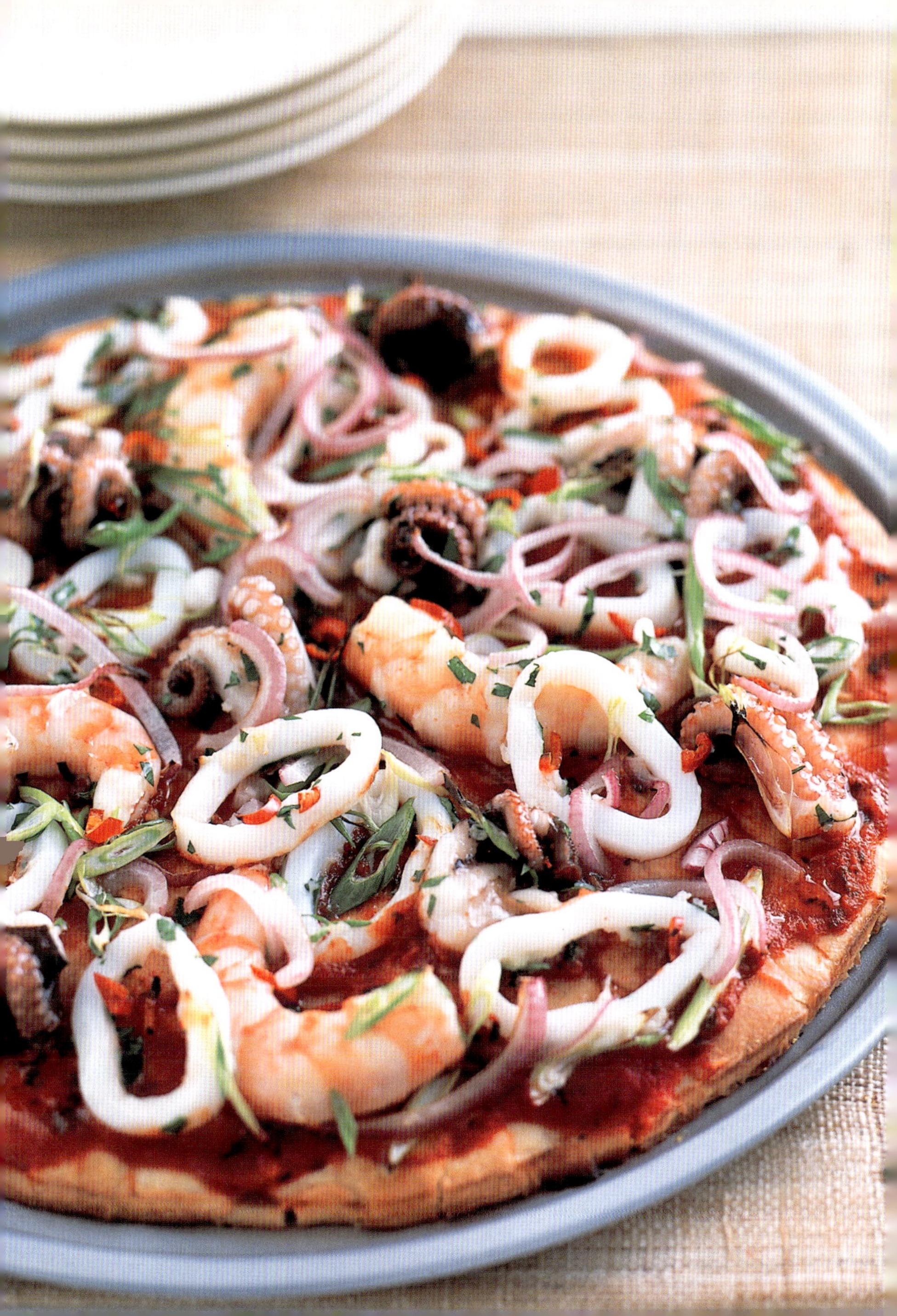

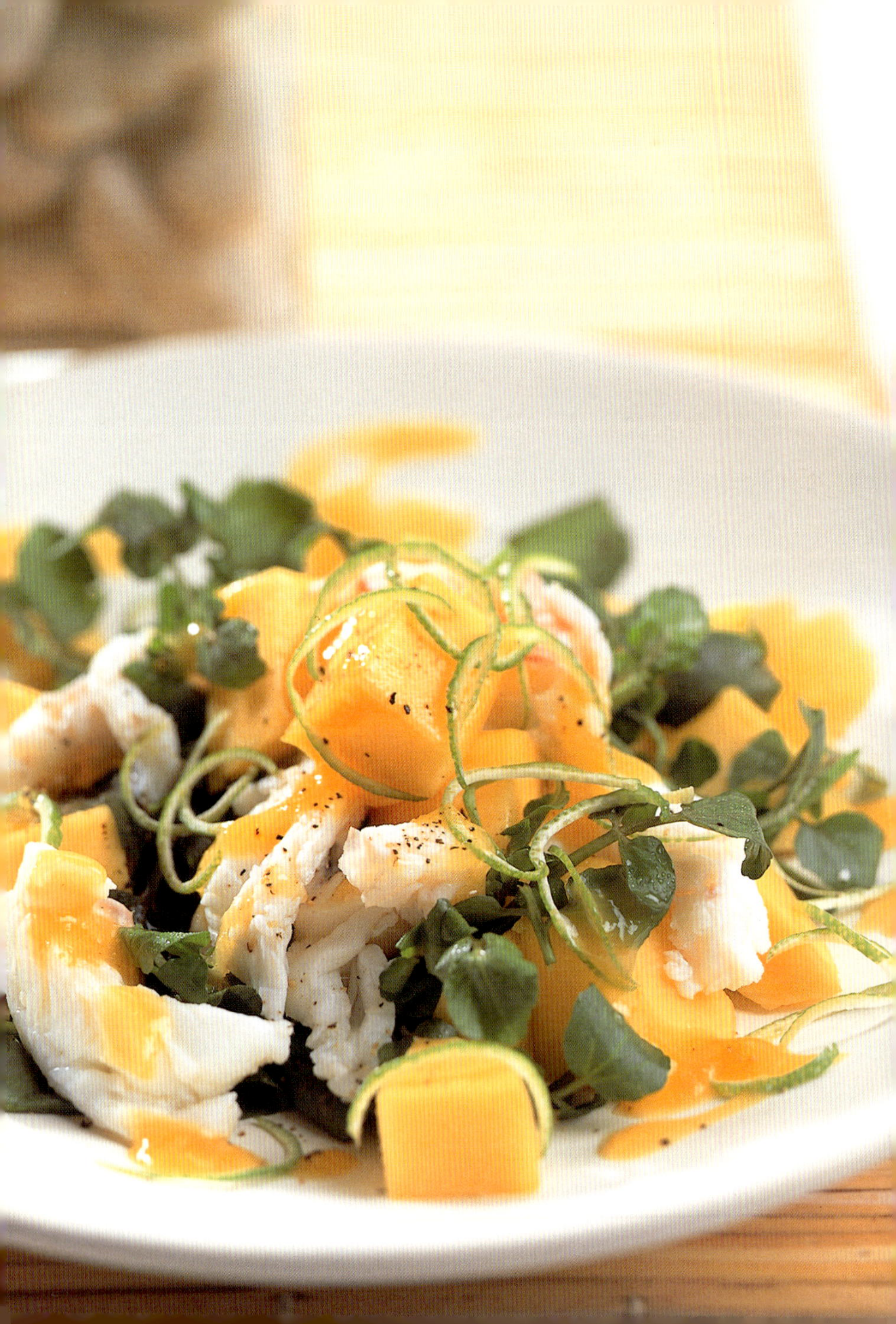

balmain bug with green mango salad

With similar flesh to lobster, this shovel-shaped mollusc is found along the south-east coast of Australia. You could substitute prawns or scampi in this recipe. Green mango is the tart, unripe fruit used in India, Malaysia and Thailand.

16 cooked balmain bugs (2kg)
2 medium green mangoes (860g)
80g trimmed watercress
2 tablespoons thinly sliced lime rind
fresh mango dressing
2 small ripe mangoes (600g)
1/3 cup (75g) firmly packed brown sugar
2 tablespoons grated ginger
1/3 cup (80ml) lime juice

Place balmain bugs on a board, back facing board. Cut tail from body. Cut through tail lengthways. Remove back vein from tail. Remove meat from tail halves.
Peel green mangoes; slice off cheeks. Cut mango flesh into 2cm pieces.
Combine flesh from bugs in large bowl with mango, watercress and rind; gently toss. Serve drizzled with fresh mango dressing.
Fresh mango dressing Peel mangoes, slice off cheeks; blend or process mango flesh until smooth. Combine mango puree, sugar, ginger and juice in small saucepan; cook, stirring, over low heat until sugar dissolves. Bring to a boil; simmer, uncovered, about 5 minutes or until dressing thickens slightly. Strain dressing over small bowl; discard solids in sieve, cool.

serves 4
per serving 2.8g fat; 1944kJ (465 cal)

lemon grass and lime fish parcels

The lemon grass in this dish is not eaten, but it produces an amazing aroma and flavour simply by being close to the fish during cooking.

2 lemon grass stems
$1/2$ cup chopped fresh coriander
1 teaspoon grated fresh ginger
3 cloves garlic, crushed
4 spring onions (100g), sliced thinly
2 fresh red thai chillies, seeded, chopped finely
4 firm white fish fillets (1kg)
1 lime, sliced thinly
1 tablespoon peanut oil

Trim lemon grass into 10cm pieces; cut each piece in half lengthways.
Combine, coriander, ginger, garlic, onion and chilli in small bowl.
Divide lemon grass among four pieces of foil; top with fish. Top fish with coriander mixture and lime; drizzle with oil. Fold foil around fish to enclose completely.
Cook parcels on heated grill plate (or in moderate oven) about 15 minutes or until fish is cooked through.
To serve, remove fish from foil and discard lemon grass. Serve with steamed rice and lime slices, if desired.

serves 4
per serving 10.3g fat; 1292kJ (309 cal)
tip The fish can be wrapped in blanched banana leaves instead of foil, if desired.

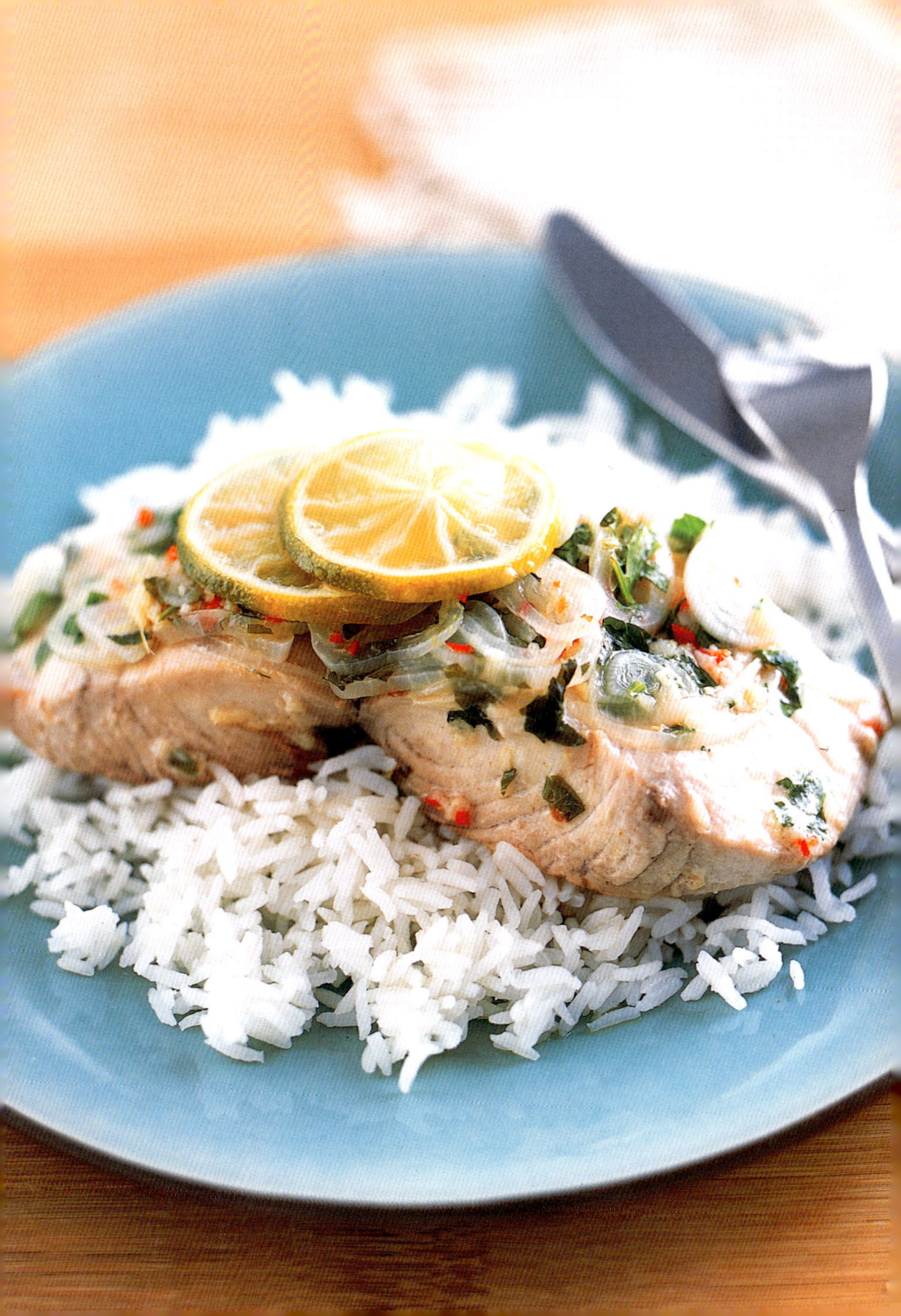

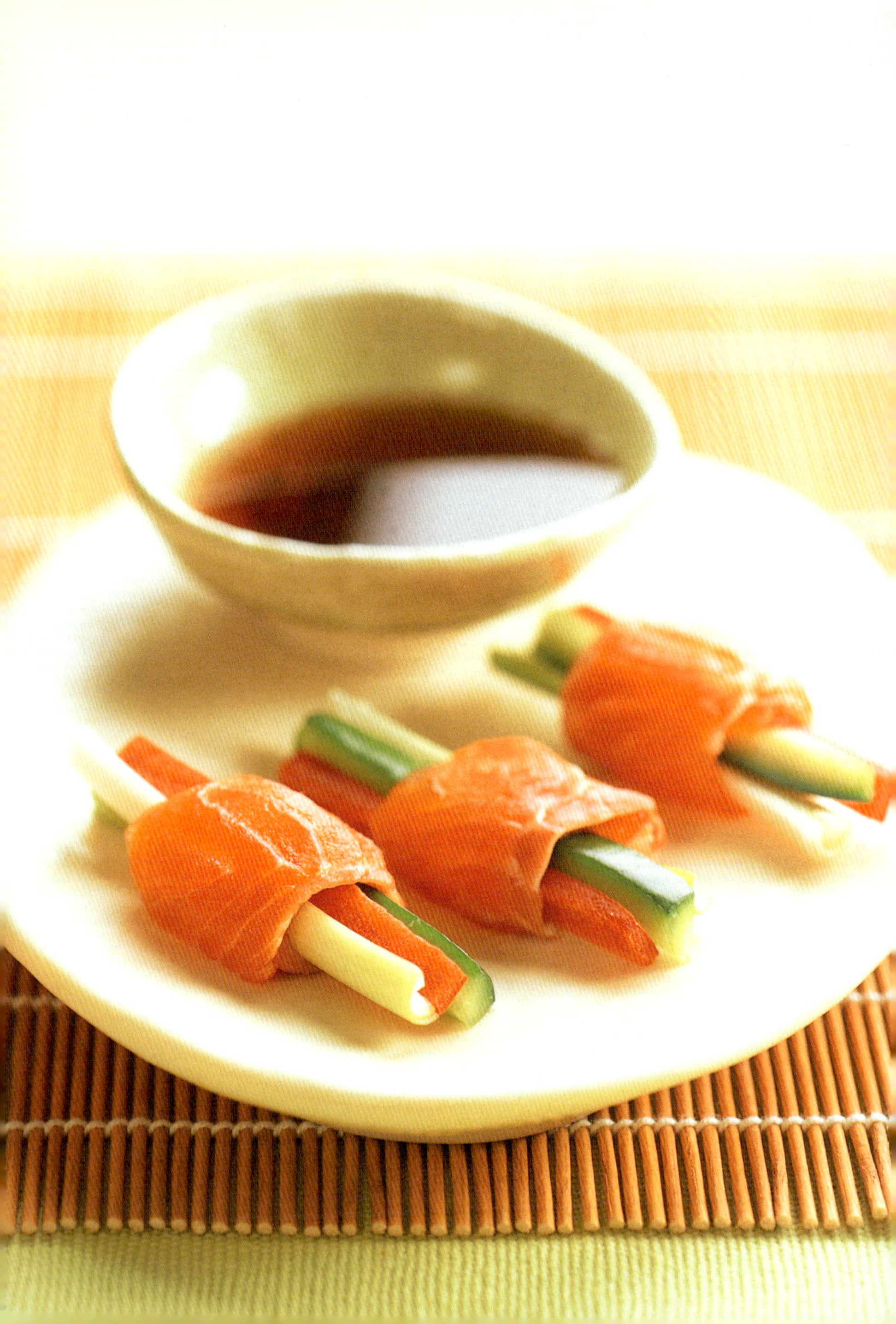

ocean trout sashimi rolls

Ocean trout sold as sashimi ocean trout has met stringent guidelines regarding its treatment since leaving the water, so you can be guaranteed of its quality and that it's safe to eat raw.

200g sashimi ocean trout
1/4 medium red capsicum (50g)
1/2 lebanese cucumber (65g)
1 green onion, trimmed
lemon dipping sauce
1/2 cup (125ml) rice vinegar
1/4 cup (55g) caster sugar
2 teaspoons light soy sauce
1/2 teaspoon finely grated lemon rind

Using sharp knife, cut trout into paper-thin slices (you need 16 slices).
Remove and discard seeds and membranes from capsicum; halve cucumber lengthways, scoop out seeds. Halve onion lengthways. Slice capsicum, cucumber and onion into 8cm-long pieces.
Lay trout slices on board in single layer; divide capsicum, cucumber and onion among trout slices, mounding at one of the narrow edges. Roll slices around filling; place rolls, seam-side down, on platter and serve immediately with lemon dipping sauce.
Lemon dipping sauce Heat vinegar, sugar and sauce in small saucepan, stirring, until sugar dissolves. Remove from heat, add rind; stand 10 minutes. Strain sauce into serving bowl; discard rind.

makes 16
per roll 0.5g fat; 64kJ (15 cal)
per tablespoon sauce 0g fat; 121kJ (29 cal)

clams with tomato vinaigrette

Live clams are often sold "sand-free" and need no preparation. To clean clams, scrub shells with stiff brush if necessary, then soak in lightly salted water for a few hours; stir occasionally, or change the water, to encourage them to discard their sand.

2.5kg clams, prepared
½ cup (125ml) dry white wine
1 small red onion (100g), chopped finely
2 cloves garlic, crushed
2 tablespoons lemon juice
2 tablespoons white wine vinegar
½ cup (125ml) olive oil
5 large tomatoes (1.25kg), chopped coarsely
4 green onions, sliced finely
2 tablespoons chopped fresh coriander

Rinse clams under cold water; drain. Place clams in large saucepan with wine, cover, bring to boil; simmer about 5 minutes or until shells open (discard any that do not).
Meanwhile, heat oiled large frying pan; cook red onion and garlic over medium heat until lightly browned. Add combined juice, vinegar and oil; cook, stirring, about 2 minutes or until thickened slightly.
Drain clams; discard liquid.
Gently toss clams with tomato, green onion, coriander and red onion mixture.

serves 4
per serving 30.7g fat; 1584kJ (379 cal)
tip Water can be used in place of white wine, if desired.

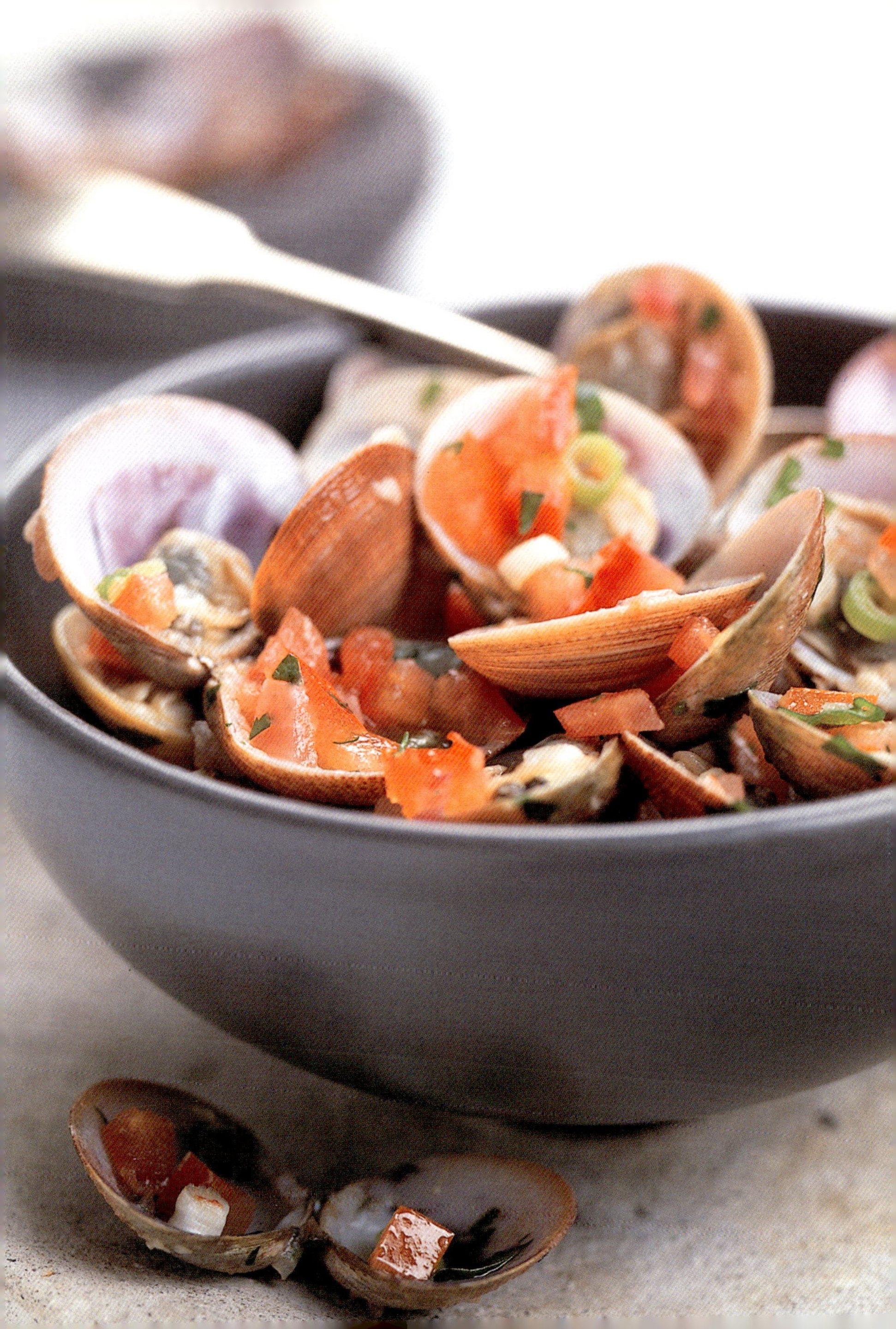

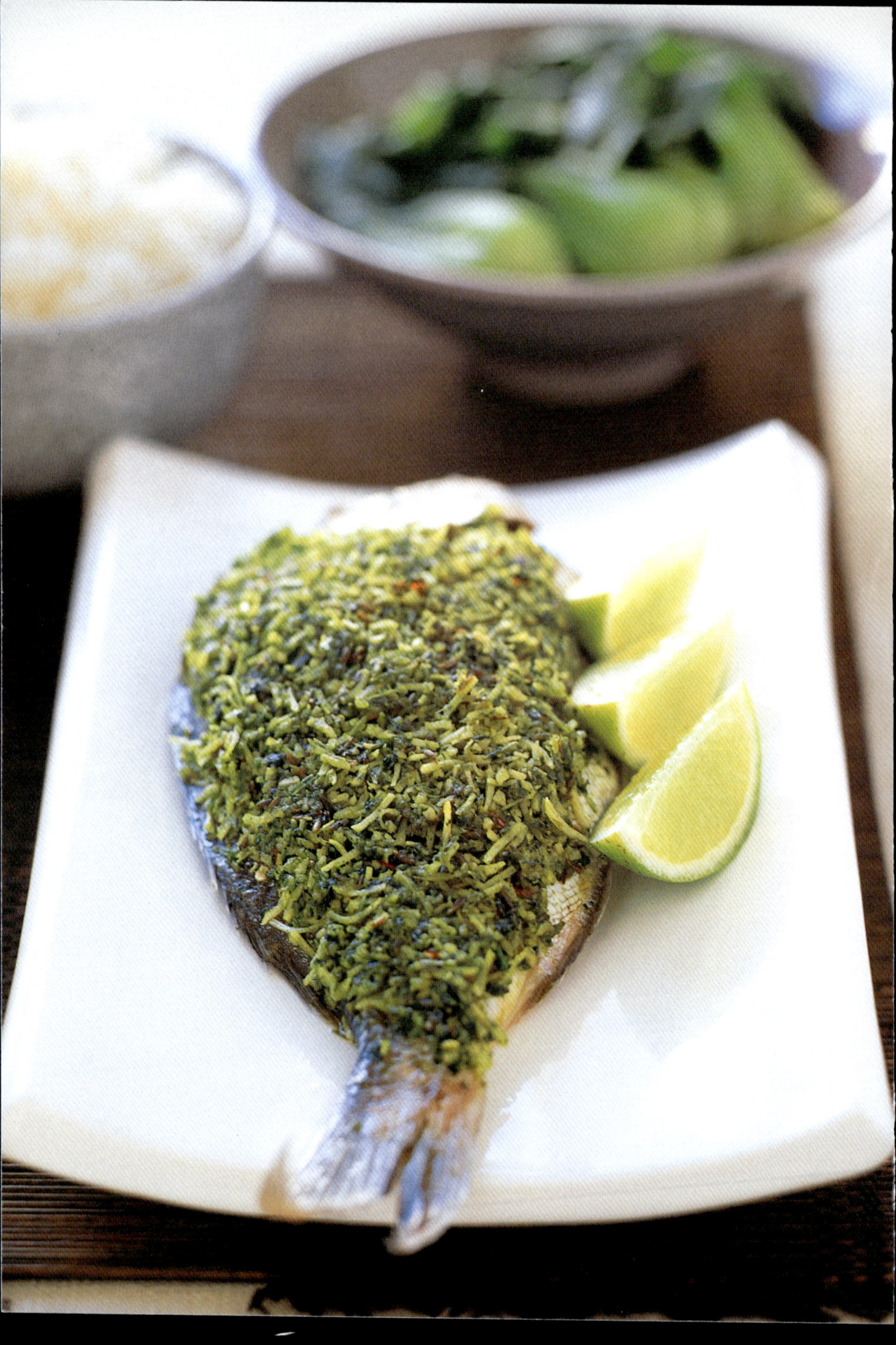

steamed coconut fish

We used snapper in this recipe, but you can use any whole white-fleshed fish, such as bream or flathead. You will need a piece of ginger about 3cm long for this recipe.

2 cups chopped fresh coriander
2 fresh red thai chillies, chopped coarsely
2 cloves garlic, quartered
20g fresh ginger, peeled, chopped coarsely
1 tablespoon cumin seeds
²/₃ cup (50g) shredded coconut
1 tablespoon peanut oil
4 medium whole snapper (1.8kg)

Blend or process coriander, chilli, garlic, ginger and seeds until chopped finely.
Combine coriander mixture with coconut and oil in small bowl; mix well.
Score each fish three times on both sides; place each fish on a large sheet of foil. Press coconut mixture onto fish; fold foil over to enclose fish.
Place fish in large bamboo steamer; steam fish, covered, over wok or large saucepan of simmering water about 25 minutes or until cooked through.
Serve with steamed rice, stir-fried baby bok choy and lime wedges, if desired.

serves 4
per serving 15.8g fat; 1237kJ (296 cal)
tip Prick the foil with a skewer to allow the steam to escape.

five-spice calamari

1kg whole small calamari
$\frac{1}{2}$ cup (75g) plain flour
$\frac{1}{4}$ cup (55g) crushed
   sea salt flakes or
   1 tablespoon sea salt
1$\frac{1}{2}$ tablespoons ground
   white pepper
1 tablespoon five-spice
   powder
1$\frac{1}{2}$ teaspoons
   chilli powder
vegetable oil, for
   deep-frying

Clean calamari by gently pulling head and tentacles away from body. Remove clear backbone (quill) from inside body. Cut tentacles from head just below eyes; discard head. Remove side fins and skin from body with salted fingers. Rinse body, tentacles and fins if necessary.

Cut body to open out flat. Using a sharp knife, lightly score inside flesh in a diagonal pattern. Cut tentacles into pieces and fins into strips. Pat calamari dry on absorbent paper.

Combine flour, salt, pepper, five-spice and chilli in large bowl.

Add a small handful of calamari to flour mixture and toss to coat. Deep-fry calamari in hot oil until browned lightly and crisp. Drain well on absorbent paper. Repeat with remaining calamari and flour mixture.

serves 4
per serving 18.4g fat; 1651kJ (395 cal)
tip Calamari is best eaten as soon as it is cooked, but can be kept warm, on an absorbent-paper-covered tray, in a very slow oven while cooking in batches.

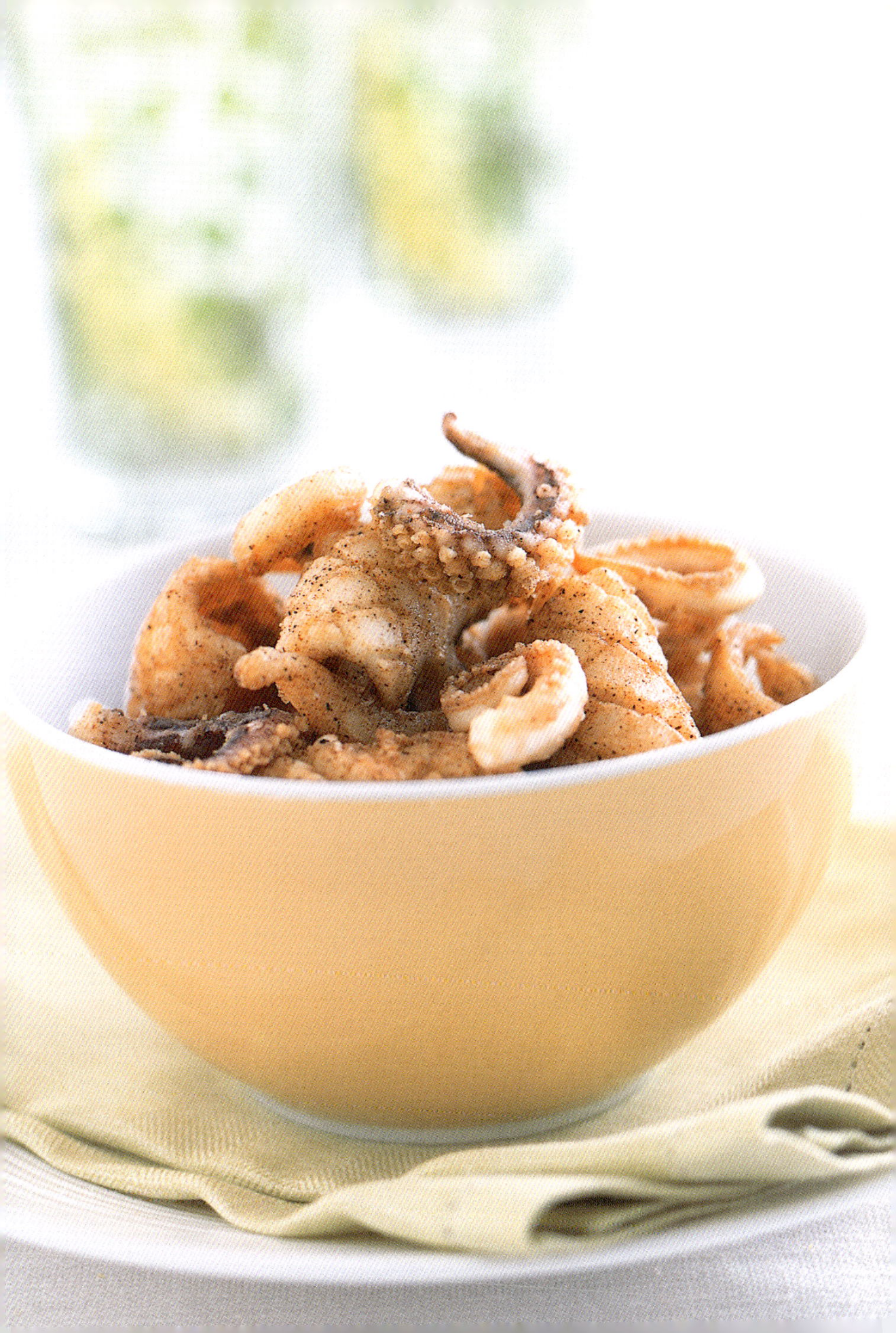

glossary

balmain bug shovel-shaped mollusc with flesh similar to that of a lobster.

bean thread noodles also known as cellophane or glass noodles because they are transparent when cooked; made from extruded mung bean paste. White in colour and very fine; available dried in various-sized bundles. Must be soaked to soften before use; using them deep-fried requires no pre-soaking.

blue swimmer crab also known as sand crabs and atlantic blue crabs.

calamari a type of squid.

capers the grey-green buds of a warm-climate (usually Mediterranean) shrub, sold either dried and salted or pickled in a vinegar brine; tiny young ones, called baby capers, are also available.

capsicum also known as bell pepper or, simply, pepper. Native to Central and South America, they can be red, green, yellow, orange or purplish black. Discard seeds and membranes before use.

chillies
  dutch: long, medium-hot, but flavoursome, fresh chilli; also known as a holland chilli.
  jalapeño: fairly hot green chilli, available in brine, bottled or canned, or fresh from specialty greengrocers.
  powder: the Asian variety, made from dried ground thai chillies, is the hottest; use as a substitute for fresh chillies in proportion of ½ teaspoon ground chilli powder to 1 medium fresh chilli.
  red thai: small, hot, and bright red in colour.

chinese cabbage also known as peking or napa cabbage, wong bok and petsai.

clams bivalve mollusc; also known as vongole. We used a small ridge-shelled variety.

coconut, shredded thin strips of dried coconut.

coriander also known as pak chee, cilantro or chinese parsley; bright-green leafy herb with a pungent flavour. Both the stems and roots of coriander are also used in Thai cooking. Coriander seeds are also available, but are no substitute for fresh coriander, as the taste is very different.

crab meat flesh of fresh crabs.

cumin seeds also known as zeera.

fish sauce also known as nam pla or nuoc nam; made from pulverised, salted, fermented fish (most often anchovies); has a pungent smell and strong taste. There are many versions of varying intensity, so use according to your taste.

five-spice powder fragrant ground mixture of cinnamon, clove, star anise, sichuan pepper and fennel seeds.

flour, plain an all-purpose flour, made from wheat.

garlic salt packaged mixture of finely powdered garlic and table salt.

ginger also known as green or root ginger; thick gnarled root of a tropical plant. Can be kept, peeled, covered with sherry in a jar, and refrigerated or frozen in an airtight container.

lebanese cucumber long, slender and thin-skinned; also known as the european or burpless cucumber.

lemon grass a tall, clumping, lemon-smelling and -tasting, sharp-edged grass; the white lower part of the stem is used, finely chopped, in cooking.

lemon pepper seasoning a blend of crushed black pepper, lemon, herbs and spices.

mango tropical fruit originally from India or South-East Asia, with skin colour ranging from green through yellow to deep red. Fragrant yellow flesh surrounds a large flat seed.

mayonnaise we use whole-egg mayonnaise in our recipes.

mirin Japanese champagne-coloured cooking wine made of glutinous rice and alcohol; used expressly for cooking and should not be confused with sake.

mussels, black purchase from a fish market where fish is reliably fresh. They must be tightly closed when bought, indicating they are alive. Before cooking, scrub shells with a strong brush and remove the "beards". Discard mussels that do not open during cooking.

oil
  olive: made from ripened olives. Extra virgin and virgin are the best while extra light or light refers to the taste not fat levels.
  peanut: pressed from ground peanuts; most commonly used oil in Asian cooking because of its high smoke point (capacity to handle high heat without burning).

sesame: made from roasted, crushed, white sesame seeds; used as a flavouring rather than a cooking medium.
vegetable: any of a number of oils sourced from plants rather than animal fats.

onion
green: also known as scallion or, incorrectly, shallot; young onion picked before the bulb has formed, having a long, bright-green edible stalk.
red: also known as spanish, red spanish or bermuda onion; a sweet-flavoured, large, purple-red onion.
spring: have crisp, narrow, green-leafed tops and fairly large sweet white bulb.

paprika ground dried red capsicum (bell pepper); available sweet or hot.

parmesan cheese also known as parmigiano; a hard, grainy cow-milk cheese originating in the Parma region of Italy. The curd is salted in brine before being aged up to two years.

parsley, flat-leaf also known as continental or italian parsley.

polenta flour-like cereal made of ground corn (maize); similar to cornmeal, but finer and lighter in colour. Also the name of the dish made from it.

prawns also known as shrimp.

radicchio burgundy-leaved lettuce with slightly bitter flavour.

rice paper rounds also known as banh trang. Made from rice paste and stamped into rounds. Dipped momentarily in water, they become pliable wrappers for fried food and uncooked vegetables. Make good spring-roll wrappers.

rice wine cooking rice wine is rice wine with salt added; sherry can be substituted.

rocket also known as arugula, rugula and rucola; a peppery-tasting green leaf. Baby rocket leaves are both smaller and less peppery.

sashimi skinless, boneless raw fish pieces.

sesame seeds black and white are the most common of these tiny oval seeds.

soy sauce also known as sieu; made from fermented soy beans. Several variations are available in supermarkets and Asian food stores.

spinach also known as english spinach and, incorrectly, silverbeet.

sprouts also known as bean shoots; tender new growths of beans and seeds germinated for consumption as sprouts. The most readily available are mung bean, soy bean, alfalfa and snow pea sprouts.

squid hoods type of mollusc; also known as calamari. Buy squid hoods to make preparation easier.

stock 1 cup (250ml) stock is equivalent to 1 cup (250ml) water plus 1 stock cube (or 1 teaspoon stock powder).

sugar we used coarse, granulated table sugar, also known as crystal sugar, unless otherwise specified.
brown: an extremely soft, fine, granulated sugar retaining molasses for its characteristic colour and flavour.
caster: also known as superfine or finely granulated table sugar.

sweet chilli sauce made from red chillies, sugar, garlic and vinegar; used as a condiment as well as in cooking.

tomato
cherry: also known as tiny tim or tom thumb tomatoes; small and round.
egg: also called plum or roma, these are smallish, oval-shaped tomatoes.
pizza sauce: commercially packaged tomato sauce used to spread over pizza bases.

vinegar
balsamic: authentic only from the province of Modena, Italy; made from a regional wine of white Trebbiano grapes specially processed then aged in antique wooden casks to give the exquisite pungent flavour.
red wine: based on fermented red wine.
rice: a colourless vinegar made from fermented rice and flavoured with sugar and salt. Also known as seasoned rice vinegar.
white: made from spirit of cane sugar.
white wine: made from white wine.

wasabi an Asian horseradish sold as a powder or paste.

watercress one of the cress family; a large group of peppery greens used raw in salads, sandwiches and dips, or cooked in soups. Highly perishable, so must be used as soon as possible after purchase.

wine we used good-quality dry white and red wines in our recipes.

61

conversion chart

MEASURES

One Australian metric measuring cup holds approximately 250ml, one Australian metric tablespoon holds 20ml, one Australian metric teaspoon holds 5ml.

The difference between one country's measuring cups and another's is within a two- or three-teaspoon variance, and will not affect your cooking results. North America, New Zealand and the United Kingdom use a 15ml tablespoon.

All cup and spoon measurements are level. The most accurate way of measuring dry ingredients is to weigh them. When measuring liquids, use a clear glass or plastic jug with the metric markings.

We use large eggs with an average weight of 60g.

OVEN TEMPERATURES

These oven temperatures are only a guide for conventional ovens. For fan-forced ovens, check the manufacturer's manual.

	°C (CELSIUS)	°F (FAHRENHEIT)	GAS MARK
Very slow	120	250	½
Slow	150	275 – 300	1 – 2
Moderately slow	160	325	3
Moderate	180	350 – 375	4 – 5
Moderately hot	200	400	6
Hot	220	425 – 450	7 – 8
Very hot	240	475	9

DRY MEASURES

METRIC	IMPERIAL
15g	½oz
30g	1oz
60g	2oz
90g	3oz
125g	4oz (¼lb)
155g	5oz
185g	6oz
220g	7oz
250g	8oz (½lb)
280g	9oz
315g	10oz
345g	11oz
375g	12oz (¾lb)
410g	13oz
440g	14oz
470g	15oz
500g	16oz (1lb)
750g	24oz (1½lb)
1kg	32oz (2lb)

LIQUID MEASURES

METRIC	IMPERIAL
30ml	1 fluid oz
60ml	2 fluid oz
100ml	3 fluid oz
125ml	4 fluid oz
150ml	5 fluid oz (¼ pint/1 gill)
190ml	6 fluid oz
250ml	8 fluid oz
300ml	10 fluid oz (½ pint)
500ml	16 fluid oz
600ml	20 fluid oz (1 pint)
1000ml (1 litre)	1¾ pints

LENGTH MEASURES

METRIC	IMPERIAL
3mm	⅛in
6mm	¼in
1cm	½in
2cm	¾in
2.5cm	1in
5cm	2in
6cm	2½in
8cm	3in
10cm	4in
13cm	5in
15cm	6in
18cm	7in
20cm	8in
23cm	9in
25cm	10in
28cm	11in
30cm	12in (1ft)

index

aïoli, lime, prawn cocktail with 9
asparagus, prawn
 and sesame stir-fry 29

balmain bug with
 green mango salad 49

calamari rings with
 chermoulla 37
calamari, five-spice 58
carpaccio, tuna, with lemon oil
 and baby capers 14
ceviche 22
chermoulla, calamari
 rings with 37
chilli and garlic octopus 6
chilli crab 26
chilli prawn and noodle salad 18
chilli scallops 17
chilli seafood pizza 46
clams with tomato vinaigrette 54
coconut fish, steamed 57
coriander pesto,
 swordfish with 30
crab, chilli 26
crab, thai, radicchio
 salad cups 41
crisp-skinned thai
 chilli snapper 5
cucumber salad, salt and
 pepper squid with 21

fish kebabs, spicy 10
fish parcels, lemon grass
 and lime 50
fish, coconut, steamed 57
five-spice calamari 58
fresh rice paper rolls
 with prawns 38

garlic prawns, stir-fried 25

green mango salad,
 balmain bug with 49

kebabs, spicy fish 10

lemon grass and lime
 fish parcels 50
lemon prawns, skewered 2
lime aïoli, prawn cocktail with 9

mango salad, green,
 balmain bug with 49
marinated octopus salad 13
mussels, steamed, with
 chilli and coriander 42

noodle salad, chilli prawn and 18

ocean trout sashimi rolls 53
octopus, chilli and garlic 6
octopus salad, marinated 13
oysters osaka 45

pesto, coriander,
 swordfish with 30
pistou, rocket, prawns with 34
pizza, chilli seafood 46
prawn cocktail with lime aïoli 9
prawn, asparagus and
 sesame stir-fry 29
prawn, chilli, and noodle salad 18
prawns with rocket pistou 34
prawns, fresh rice paper
 rolls with 38
prawns, garlic, stir-fried 25
prawns, lemon, skewered 2

radicchio salad cups,
 thai crab 41
rice paper rolls with
 prawns, fresh 38

rocket pistou, prawns with 34

salad cups, radicchio,
 thai crab 41
salad, chilli prawn
 and noodle 18
salad, cucumber, salt and
 pepper squid with 21
salad, green mango,
 balmain bug with 49
salad, marinated octopus 13
salt and pepper squid
 with cucumber salad 21
sashimi rolls, ocean trout 53
scallops, chilli 17
scallops, tarragon and lime 33
seafood pizza, chilli 46
skewered lemon prawns 2
snapper, thai chilli,
 crisp-skinned 5
spicy fish kebabs 10
squid, salt and pepper,
 with cucumber salad 21
steamed coconut fish 57
steamed mussels with
 chilli and coriander 42
stir-fried garlic prawns 25
stir-fry, prawn, asparagus
 and sesame 29
swordfish with
 coriander pesto 30

tarragon and lime scallops 33
thai chilli snapper,
 crisp-skinned 5
thai crab radicchio
 salad cups 41
tomato vinaigrette,
 clams with 54
tuna carpaccio with lemon
 oil and baby capers 14

Are you missing some of the world's favourite cookbooks?

The Australian Women's Weekly cookbooks are available from bookshops, cookshops, supermarkets and other stores all over the world. You can also buy direct from the publisher, using the order form below.

MINI SERIES £3.50   190x138MM   64 PAGES

TITLE	QTY	TITLE	QTY	TITLE	QTY
4 Fast Ingredients		Dried Fruit & Nuts		Party Food	
15-minute Feasts		Drinks		Pasta	
30-minute Meals		Fast Food for Friends		Pickles and Chutneys	
50 Fast Chicken Fillets		Fast Soup		Potatoes	
50 Fast Desserts (Oct 06)		Finger Food		Risotto	
After-work Stir-fries		Gluten-free Cooking		Roast	
Barbecue		Healthy Everyday Food 4 Kids		Salads	
Barbecue Chicken		Ice-creams & Sorbets		Simple Slices	
Barbecued Seafood		Indian Cooking		Simply Seafood	
Biscuits, Brownies & Biscotti		Indonesian Favourites		Skinny Food	
Bites		Italian		Spanish Favourites	
Bowl Food		Italian Favourites		Stir-fries	
Burgers, Rösti & Fritters		Jams & Jellies		Summer Salads	
Cafe Cakes		Japanese Favourites		Tapas, Antipasto & Mezze	
Cafe Food		Kids Party Food		Thai Cooking	
Casseroles		Last-minute Meals		Thai Favourites	
Char-grills & Barbecues		Lebanese Cooking		The Fast Egg	
Cheesecakes, Pavlova & Trifles		Low Fat Fast		The Packed Lunch	
Chinese Favourites		Malaysian Favourites		Vegetarian	
Chocolate Cakes		Mince		Vegetarian Stir-fries	
Christmas Cakes & Puddings		Mince Favourites		Vegie Main Meals	
Cocktails		Muffins		Wok	
Crumbles & Bakes		Noodles		Young Chef	
Curries		Outdoor Eating		TOTAL COST	£

Photocopy and complete coupon below

ACP Magazines Ltd Privacy Notice
This book may contain offers, competitions or surveys that require you to provide information about yourself if you choose to enter or take part in any such Reader Offer.
If you provide information about yourself to ACP Magazines Ltd, the company will use this information to provide you with the products or services you have requested, and may supply your information to contractors that help ACP to do this. ACP will also use your information to inform you of other ACP publications, products, services and events. ACP will also give your information to organisations that are providing special prizes or offers, and that are clearly associated with the Reader Offer.
Unless you tell us not to, we may give your information to other organisations that use it to inform you about other products, services and events or who may give it to other organisations that may use it for this purpose. If you would like to gain access to the information ACP holds about you, please contact ACP's Privacy Officer at:
ACP Magazines Ltd, 54-58 Park Street, Sydney, NSW 2000, Australia

☐ Privacy Notice: Please do not provide information about me to any organisation not associated with this offer.

Name _____
Address _____
_____ Postcode _____
Country _____ Phone (business hours) _____
Email*(optional) _____
* By including your email address, you consent to receipt of any email regarding this magazine, and other emails which inform you of ACP's other publications, products, services and events, and to promote third party goods and services you may be interested in.

I enclose my cheque/money order for £ _____ or please charge £ _____
to my: ☐ Access ☐ Mastercard ☐ Visa ☐ Diners Club
PLEASE NOTE: WE DO NOT ACCEPT SWITCH OR ELECTRON CARDS
Card number | | | | | | | | | | | | | | | |

3 digit security code *(found on reverse of card)* _____
Cardholder's
signature _____ Expiry date ___/___

To order: Mail or fax – photocopy or complete the order form above, and send your credit card details or cheque payable to: Australian Consolidated Press (UK), Moulton Park Business Centre, Red House Road, Moulton Park, Northampton NN3 6AQ, phone (+44) (01) 604 497531, fax (+44) (01) 604 497533, e-mail books@acpmedia.co.uk. Or order online at www.acpuk.com
Non-UK residents: We accept the credit cards listed on the coupon, or cheques, drafts or International Money Orders payable in sterling and drawn on a UK bank. Credit card charges are at the exchange rate current at the time of payment.
All prices current at time of going to press and subject to change/availability.
Postage and packing UK: Add £1.00 per order plus 25p per book.
Postage and packing overseas: Add £2.00 per order plus 50p per book. **Offer ends 31.12.2007**